Above: Sunset on old wharf piles symbolises the final sunset on
Onekaka's iron industry. Ore mined from hills above Golden Bay
was smelted to produce iron. The metal was loaded into ships at
this wharf. The venture prospered in the 1920s, then declined.
It staggered on until the mid-1950s.

Published by Sandfly Publishing
85 Moncks Spur Road
Redcliffs
Christchurch 8081 New Zealand

Designed by Smartwork Creative, www.smartworkcreative.co.nz
Printed in China by Everbest Printing Co Ltd

First published by Sandfly Publishing 2016

ISBN 978-0-473-34935-6

TALES FROM THE BACKROADS

A journey through the South Island's Heartland

WRITTEN BY MIKE CREAN
PHOTOGRAPHY BY DAVID HALLETT

SANDFLY
PUBLISHING

Viaducts and tunnels on the former Otago Central railway
corridor add excitement for riders on the rail trail. The trail
was developed on the 150 kilometre-long Middlemarch-Clyde
section of line after the railway closed in 1990.

Contents

Left: Dutch explorer Abel Tasman called this "a land uplifted high".
New Zealand's tallest peaks, Mt Cook at right of centre and
Mt Tasman at left, soar above Gillespies Beach, near Fox Glacier.
In World War II this remote beach was surveyed as a potential
source of uranium for the United States' nuclear bomb project.

Introduction

A walking track through wet bush leads me, slipping and sliding in street shoes, to a series of limestone caves in the side of a hill.

Less than a year has passed since the Canterbury earthquakes. Aftershocks are still rattling walls and windows. So I feel no inclination to probe the confined spaces of caves.

It is late-2011. I am on a four-day trip to gather material for the Heartland columns in weekend editions of The Press newspaper.

The essence of Heartland was my personal impressions of country places around the South Island. It was a light-hearted, chatty blend of history, folk lore, geography, current events and interesting characters.

I hope the columns were informative but do not claim them to have been authoritative. They contained the views of local residents, rather than the histories that dwell in books.

Heartland columns came from places I had always wanted to see, places that others had suggested, places that had popped into the news, places that I just happened to come across on my Heartland journeys. In all, more than 400 places (a few of them done twice) over 10 years of travels, plus about 30 in the North Island.

The limestone caves are up a back road in East Otago. I have driven probably 100 times past a road sign pointing to Trotters Gorge and wondered what was up the road that snaked into the hills. On this trip I turn off the highway to find out.

Not far up the road I find a camping ground in a pleasant gully surrounded by native vegetation. A house bus stands there, its owner relaxing in a deck chair beside it. We get chatting. She is from the North Island and knows little about the place – except for the caves. She has hiked up to them and recommends the track to me.

It has been raining and the ground is mucky, with many puddles. But it is worth getting a bit muddy to see the caves. Forty minutes later I am back at the camping ground. In the car again, I follow the road up Trotters Creek gorge, below a limestone escarpment. The road then descends to flat farm lands before entering the town of Palmerston by the "back door".

This short drive is an ideal detour for travellers wanting an escape from endless highway traffic. The road is sealed and the gradient is easy.

I find some information on Scottish immigrant William Trotter in the Dunedin Public Library. He worked for whaling captain Johnny Jones at Waikouaiti before taking up the pastoral run that included the gorge to which his name became attached.

Trotter later bought farms in Southland. He achieved renown among runholders for driving sheep from his coastal East Otago station to present-day Frankton, near Queenstown.

Travelling, researching and writing about rural places was the most enjoyable "work" I can imagine. I treasured hearing readers of The Press say they enjoyed a column so much they went and visited the place themselves.

Another form of reader response was: "Are you going to compile your columns into a book?"

After discussing this with respective Press editors, who were all supportive, I decided not to compile columns. Rather, I would identify themes common to rural South Island and choose places that typified these themes. The Heartland columns would be a resource from which to draw characters and stories that had enchanted me.

This book is the result. I hope the stories and characters enchant you too.

My thanks go to friend and former Press colleague David Hallett who took most of the photographs with his well known expertise. Thanks also to Press staff who encouraged me to get out on the back roads and "do my thing", especially current editor Joanna Norris whose enthusiasm boosted me.

Special thanks to my wife, Margaret. In the last few years of Heartland she accompanied me on some trips. She managed to goad me into approaching strangers and getting them talking. That is something this shy little Hawarden boy always found daunting.

I want to thank Heartland readers too, especially those who responded, mostly with positive comments. The occasional complaint surfaced. One reader corrected my loose assertion that Garston was "halfway between Lumsden and Kingston" and produced the exact distances in kilometres.

So please remember, this book is not authoritative. I have tried to be accurate but some accounts of events may vary from strict history. They are drawn from the understandings that local people have. It is a sort of oral history, which I find appealing.

Remember, too, the Heartland columns are up to 10 years old. Some details may have changed since I wrote them. However, I have chosen to relate stories from my travels in the present tense, in the hope that readers may find a sense of immediacy in them.

Mike Crean, January, 2016.

Built of concrete and sited on a low hill, the Kelso dairy factory survived huge floods that struck the town in 1978 and 1980. The second flood was one too many for the West Otago farming town. Businesses closed and nearly all the residents moved away permanently.

CHAPTER 1

Old gold

FOUL CURSES RANG OUT as Henry Garrett and his mates dragged themselves dripping from the Taieri River.

At least, that is how I imagine the scene, on the Taieri Plain, just south of Dunedin. For Garrett was an outlaw and a bandit. He has been referred to as New Zealand's first bushranger; our own Ned Kelly.

Garrett was known to have associated with Richard Burgess who, with other evil mates, plundered and murdered lonely gold diggers in Westland and Nelson. Burgess and two others were hanged for their crimes.

Garrett gathered a gang of thugs around him and robbed a gun store in Dunedin, a small settlement then but soon to explode with grog houses, stores and banks as wealth poured in from the Otago gold rushes. The year was 1861. Tasmanian prospector Gabriel Read had recently discovered gold beside the Tuapeka River. The site of his find was named after him – Gabriels Gully, which runs down to present-day Lawrence.

How Garrett and his gang came to be in Dunedin and why they were crossing the Taieri River is a story steeped in Otago history. A retired police officer who had trod the beat in working-class South Dunedin during the late 1900s contacted me and suggested I might write a Heartland column about it. He lent me a book that contained an account of Garrett's career in crime. Other references I found supported what the old copper had said.

Garrett had been arrested in his home country of England for violent crime. He had been transported to Australia and put to hard labour in the penal colony on Norfolk Island. One source I read said he had escaped from there. Another said he had been released after serving his time. Whatever, he had boarded a ship and fetched up at Dunedin.

The 13-year-old town was ringing to the call of: "One a pecker, Tuapeka, bright fine gold". Garrett and his gang wanted some of it but they would not lower themselves to digging for it. Raiding a gun shop and arming themselves with pistols rather than shovels, they set off.

The Taieri River is one of New Zealand's longest and can be treacherous to cross. The dunking that Garrett and Co got must have made them curse and swear. But they kept going, until they met the next obstacle on the journey, the massive Maungatua Hill. Maybe this was too much for the crooks to bear. They set up camp in bush at the foot of a gully. There they committed their dastardly deeds.

Opposite: The moonlit waters of the Taieri River roll sleepily towards Otago's coastal hills. But this long serpentine stream is a coiled snake, ready to pounce over its banks and flood the Taieri Plain after heavy rain in the highlands.

By late 1861 diggers had worn a track up and down this gully. New chums full of hope and laden with shovels and pans were heading up to the diggings; successful miners carrying precious nuggets in bags tied inside their coats were heading down to Dunedin to deposit their riches in the bank. Garrett's gang held up 15 returning diggers at gunpoint. They relieved their victims of their gold and tied them to trees. Then they scarpered with their loot.

They got away but, in an example of policing that would still be impressive today, Garrett was nabbed in Sydney and brought back to Dunedin for trial. He served a term of imprisonment in Dunedin, was released but re-offended and was locked up again. He completed his sentence in Lyttelton Jail.

The story made me wonder what Otago's God-fearing Presbyterian pioneers must have thought about Garrett and his gang. The book that the old cop lent me said local folk had been complaining for weeks about lawless gold seekers passing through their area, stealing and killing sheep for food. When word got around that Garrett was about, locals bolted their doors and barred their windows.

Left: Conditions on Otago's Waipori goldfields could drive a man insane. Kerri Driscoll reflects on the murder of her great-great-great grandfather by a mad miner, in 1866. Water has obliterated all signs of the crime, as the town of Waipori Junction was flooded by the creation of Lake Mahinerangi for electricity generation, in 1925. The town was just below the far bank of the lake in this picture.
Driscoll Family Collection

Left: Dunedin's need for electricity caused the drowning of a town. Waipori Junction was the business and social centre for gold miners scattered over a high plateau 30 kilometres west of the city. Damming of the Waipori River, which runs "up" the photo at right, created Lake Mahinerangi.
Driscoll Family Collection

I decided to visit the gully where the Garrett gang did their dirty deeds. The main road through Mosgiel leads in a few minutes to the Taieri River. A graceful bridge carries you high above the waters (Garrett would be envious) near the entry to the small town of Outram. Shortly after the road slips into the almost deserted village of Woodside. At the north end of the main street is the notorious gully. Today it is a pleasant public domain and picnic ground, known as Woodside Glen.

A dozen-or-so cottages remain at Woodside. One was clearly a store. Now it, and most of the others, are "cribs" (baches). One of them was the old cop's refuge. He used to retreat there when he wanted a break from enforcing the law in South Dunedin. Old school and hall buildings still stand also.

Woodside was once much more. It had a sawmill and a flour mill, a bootmaker and a baker, a general store and a Post Office. A range of tradesmen had workshops here. Woodside Hotel keeper J. Iveson ran a daily coach service to and from Dunedin. When the village's decline set in from the late-1880s, Iveson jacked his hotel up and moved it to Outram. A branch railway from Mosgiel had reached Outram and the town was beginning to prosper at Woodside's expense.

Woodside is a pretty place. It looks over the fertile Taieri Plain with its well-ordered farms and market gardens where families have made good livings for 150 years. Just up the road stands the stately Manor House, built from local bricks by Francis McDiarmid who arrived with other Otago founder settlers on immigrant ship Philip Laing in 1848.

Above: The still and well-behaved waters of the Taieri River roll gently towards Otago's coastal hills. But this long serpentine stream is a coiled snake, ready to pounce over its banks and flood the Taieri Plain after heavy rain in the highlands.

Fellow pioneers James and Catherine Fulton built the Sunday School that later became the community hall. Their grandson Jules Fulton and his friend Robert Hogan formed a contracting company in the Depression. Put their surnames together and you have Fulton Hogan, now the South Island's pre-eminent road building and maintenance company.

Garrett might have sworn and cursed awfully but his name is forgotten. Although legend records him as "New Zealand's first bushranger", he probably isn't. Research for a Heartland column about Purau, a bay on Banks Peninsula, revealed a crime story dating back to the 1840s.

Fifteen years before Garrett, three ex-convicts from Tasmania landed at Akaroa. The so-called Bluecap gang, the name presumably relating to their headgear, roamed around the scantily settled Banks Peninsula before descending on the home of the Greenwood brothers at Purau. The farming brothers had settled here before the first official shiploads of Canterbury colonists arrived. They and other early European settlers became known as "Pre-Adamites".

The Greenwoods offered their blue-capped visitors a bed for the night – and were repaid by having loaded guns pointed at them and being tied up, to the accompaniment of violent threats.

The gang then got drunk on the Greenwoods' wine supply and ransacked the house. After sobering up, they took the Greenwood's boat and got away. They were captured and imprisoned for 15 years.

Were the Bluecappers bushrangers? If so, they might have been New Zealand's first. You can decide.

Outram is an exception. Unlike many declining rural villages, this township on the Taieri Plain continues to prosper, though this evening view may suggest otherwise. The early growth of Outram, boosted by its branch railway line, spelled doom to neighbouring town Woodside.

Meanwhile, back to the gold seekers at the Tuapeka diggings. Of the lucky ones who struck riches, some then managed to avoid the bars and fleshpots that sprang up in the gold-fields canvas towns. They bought land and took up farming, they started in business, or they moved away. However, it is often said the people who made the most from gold were the merchants who followed in the diggers' wake, keen to profit from sale of meat, flour, tobacco, clothing, beer, whisky.

If Henry Garrett had continued to the Tuapeka diggings, he would have had a second river to cross. High on the plateau between Woodside and Gabriels Gully the Waipori River tumbles through a rocky landscape. Crossing it in the 1860s was no great problem, for it was then a narrow, shallow stream. It is now a lake and beneath it lie the drowned

remains of the substantial goldfields town of Waipori Junction.

A couple of prospectors trekking to the Tuapeka in 1861 paused for a break at the Waipori River. They did some panning along its banks and found gold. An influx of miners followed and tents quickly sprouted among the tussocks. A town with pubs, shops, banks and a school grew up to serve 2000 miners in the area.

Kerry Driscoll is descended from an early Waipori miner. She became interested in the history of Waipori after learning that her great-great-great-grandfather was murdered there in 1866. His killer was caught and hanged in one of the first executions at Dunedin.

Driscoll suggests the drowned town of Waipori Junction may be a suitable topic for a Heartland column. We agree to meet at the site of the former town. She arranges a local

Above: Early settlers on the Taieri Plain planted their Scottish roots on this fertile soil. This Scottish baronial manor stands near Woodside.

Above: Shunned by European society, Chinese miners at the Tuapeka gold diggings gathered for business and companionship at a China Town, outside the boom town of Lawrence. The sole remainder of their shops, homes and joss houses is the Chinese Empire Hotel, beside the highway to Central Otago.

Above: Headstones at a distance from the rest in the Lawrence Cemetery mark the graves of Chinese diggers. Some memorials were wooden but these can no longer be read. Some remains were exhumed and shipped back to China, many of these to be lost in a shipwreck.

farmer and a goldfields historian to join us in this desolate spot. They explain that the river was dammed in 1925 to create a lake that would drive hydro-electricity generation for Dunedin. Against protests from gold miners who were still working there, the lake waters steadily rose to lap over the old town. Today, only the cemetery survives, high and dry on "Boot Hill".

However, when the lake level drops a little, you can see treetops and the concrete tower of the former slaughter-house poking above the surface. You can trace house piles and bits of street kerbing at the lake's edge.

Driscoll ventures up here occasionally to "commune" with her forebears. She finds the sight of the town seeming to rise from the waters in a dry spell "mesmerising" and "spooky".

You can drive up the Waipori Gorge from Berwick on the Taieri Plain. The winding gravel road brings you past the dams and power stations to the lake. Further along, a side road goes down to a causeway and a bridge that crosses a narrow neck of the lake. From here you can see the site of the drowned town, to your left on the north bank. To your right on the north bank you can see a collection of huts where swirling smoke from chimneys carries the scent of trout sizzling in pans for anglers' lunches. The high road continues over the barren plateau to Lawrence.

Garrett never reached this place, of course. But people of real character did. Doggedness was a requirement to cope with life in the forbidding terrain and its weather cycle of harsh southerly winds bringing whiteout snow which then cleared to stiff frosts. Firewood was scarce as few trees grew here. Transport links were tenuous, making the cost of coal exorbitant and supplies of food irregular.

Historian David Still tells of a reclusive miner who ate only meat and spuds, thus earning the nickname Mutton Mulholland. He died of scurvy. Farmer Russell Knight shows me a memorial in the Waipori Junction cemetery to a relative of his, a local lad named Wilfred Knight. Wilfred left Waipori to see the world but had only reached Australia when World War I broke out. The inscription on the memorial says Knight enlisted and served in the Australian army. He became the first New Zealander killed at Gallipoli.

As at many goldfields, big companies moved in behind the diggers. They dug channels around the hills to bring water for their sluice guns. They erected stamper batteries to crush stone for the gold within. Relics of these can still be seen in the surrounding countryside.

The dusty road from Lake Waipori to Lawrence descends the last hill at a place called Wetherstons. A couple of houses are all that remain of this former goldfields town. Well – almost all. If you look closely you will find a different sort of relic here: the concrete and brick ruins of what was once Otago's most successful rural brewery.

About the time Garrett's gang was brandishing pistols at Woodside, brothers John and Will Wetherston were facing starvation at Gabriels Gully. Too many men were working claims, too few supplies were getting through, too high were the prices of food. For the Wetherston lads it was "slim pickings".

Below: Woodside Glen is a popular picnic spot half an hour outside Dunedin. But where barbecues now burn, armed bushrangers once ambushed prospectors returning from the Tuapeka diggings with bags of gold under their coats.

The brothers decided to head into the hills and shoot some wild pork. Just over a low range they found a likely looking gold prospect and did a trial dig. There they found gold. And there the town that took the name of Wetherstons was born.

Word of the brothers' strike got out and a typical gold rush town grew up. At its peak, with a population of 5000, its boisterous reputation was reflected in its label as "the hell-hole of the Otago goldfields". A store, a bank and a post office served the hundreds of miners who toiled at Wetherstons. For entertainment the miners could choose from 14 pubs, numerous gambling dens, billiard saloons and dancing halls (but no church). And there was the brewery – Benjamin Hart's Black Horse Brewery.

Wetherstons' rumbustious days are gone but I get a taste of them when Lawrence heritage enthusiast Kim Murtagh pulls on the garb of a Victorian dancing girl and conducts me on a walk through the old brewery site. She came to the area in 2004. Poking around in the overgrowth, she found the concrete and brick ruins.

Above: A leading Otago brewery once operated here. Local newcomer Kim Murtagh found the ruins of the malt house for Benjamin Hart's Black Horse Brewery overgrown with bush and scrub. She sparked a clean-up of the goldfields site at Wetherstons, near Lawrence.

A year later she led a volunteer working party, including Hart's great-grandson, to hack through a tangle of branches, bushes, briar and blackberry and reveal the brewery and malt house ruins and the still intact weatherboard house where Hart had lived.

The brewery operated into the early 20th century. Then gold ran out, people left, business declined. The Black Horse closed in 1923 and its buildings were left to moulder. Barely anyone had seen them in the last 30 years, or even knew they were there, until Murtagh found them. Her interest became a passion that immersed her in historical research.

Beer made Hart a wealthy man, Murtagh says. But he was more than a brewer and there was more than one kind of gold at Wetherstons. Hart's hobby was growing flowers, mainly daffodils. The golden glow from 14 varieties of daffodils he had planted over 25 acres of hillside became a popular attraction. Every spring special trains brought Dunedin folk on outings to picnic among the daffodils. Hundreds of visitors walked two kilometres from the Lawrence railway station to Wetherstons – three trains brought 1500 city folk in 1937 alone.

Car ownership grew in the 1950s and the train excursions stopped. Soon nobody came, though the daffodils still put on their display each spring.

Thank goodness, then, that Murtagh popped up, half a century later. Clearing the overgrowth, making paths and signs, giving talks to visiting groups have been hard work. As hard as digging for gold but with a different sort of reward – the satisfaction of bringing history alive.

From Wetherstons you can see roof tops and church spires on the north-facing hillsides of Lawrence. I lived and taught in Lawrence briefly in the 1970s and fell for its charm. But there is one aspect of its golden history that rankles with me.

Drive through the town, heading west, and on its outskirts you will find an old brick house standing uncommonly close to the highway. This building was the Chinese Empire Hotel. The paddock behind it slopes gently down to the Tuapeka Stream, about two kilometres below the point where Gabriel Read made his famous gold discovery.

On this lush paddock there once stood a China Town, where more than 30 buildings lined well formed streets, including cafes, joss houses and other business premises. Some Chinese miners lived here but many more dwelt in huts by the diggings up Gabriels Gully. This was where they came to do business, where they gathered for social occasions.

Here, as at other gold areas, Chinese miners worked over abandoned claims and found gold that the previous diggers had not reached. They built a reputation for hard work and honesty. But the European population of Lawrence did not want the "Asiatics" living and dealing among them. The Chinese were virtually banned from Lawrence. So they built their own town.

The Tuapeka Times newspaper was expressing, and hopefully exaggerating, the white community's racism when it branded the Chinese settlement "a nest of putrefaction" which was frequented by "a filth-begrimed, opium besotted horde of Mongolian monstrosities".

One man was instrumental in breaking down the wall of prejudice. Sam Chew Lain established the Chinese Empire Hotel.

Below left: Operating a power station in the mid-1900s required a sizeable staff. Workers on the Waipori station lived on site as access from Mosgiel and Dunedin, up the Waipori Gorge, was difficult. The road is better now and most of the houses are used as baches.

Below right: "Hell hole of the goldfields" – this was the tag given to Wetherstons. The short-lived gold town with 14 pubs for 500 diggers faded away to just a couple of farmyards and houses. In the background is the town of Lawrence, business hub of the Tuapeka.

Above: Heart of the goldfields: Gabriel Read launched the Otago gold rushes when he discovered gold up the gully that bears his name. The road to Gabriels Gully runs out of the picture at lower-left. This is downtown Lawrence, the lovely and historic town that grew up to serve the diggings.

He became the leader of the Chinese community and won respect in the European business community. By the 1880s, even Europeans were visiting his hotel.

The last resident of the China Town died in 1945. Not much was left of the settlement by then and what remained was soon removed or ploughed into the ground. The Chinese Empire Hotel became a family home. It serves as the sole reminder of a once busy place.

A stark indication of the racial discrimination is in the Lawrence cemetery. Shunned in a far corner, down a shaded dip in the land, lie a few remaining headstones of Chinese miners. Some graves were dug up and the miners' bodies taken home to China. Some had wooden plaques that have rotted into the ground. Stone plaques are cracked and crumbling, the writing on them, in Chinese and English, barely legible. One headstone that can be read marks the grave of Ah Sue, who died in 1883, aged 52. The pathos is palpable. I took groups of pupils there to reflect on all this and express their feelings in poetry. Some were inspired.

In contrast, near the crown of the hill a formidable concrete mausoleum reaches skyward. Here they laid Sam Chew Lain to rest – among European graves.

A decade ago, Otago University's anthropology department began a series of archaeological digs to unearth the lost China Town. I drive down in 2007 to check progress and find lecturer Chris Jacomb leading students in a search for the sites of buildings, streets, water wells and drains.

He has narrowed the search by consulting an 1882 map of the town and some old photographs. A growing collection of artefacts is evidence of the success of yet another sort of digging in a goldfield.

The university research was scheduled to be completed in time to allow a proposed tourist attraction to be built on the site. Dunedin historian Dr James Ng chairs a trust that plans a re-build of the old China Town as a drawcard for Chinese tourists visiting New Zealand.

The path from gangster Garrett, via Benjamin the brewer, to Chinese champion Sam Chew Lain – through four vanished villages, a new lake and hydro station, a modern tourist attraction that harks to the past – makes a classic Otago tale. Gabriel Read could never have dreamed of it as he gazed on gold sparkling in the ground by the Tuapeka Stream.

Left: The clang and bang of stamping batteries was a familiar sound in the goldfields. This stamper, which pounded rocks to crush them and reveal the gold within, stands as a memorial to the old-timers, beside the road to Gabriels Gully, near the intersection with the main street of Lawrence.

Below: Towards day's end, Gabriel Read sank his shovel into the ground, dug out some earth and found gold sparkling like the stars of Orion. That happened here, in Gabriels Gully, and it started the Otago gold rushes, in 1861.

CHAPTER 2

Storms, crashes, shocks and shakes

A FLOOD CAN BE a very moving affair. When they flooded the Cromwell Gorge to create a hydro scheme at Clyde, they had to move half of Cromwell town's homes and businesses onto a higher terrace.

But this was a man-made flood. Purely natural flooding inundated poor little Kelso twice in three years. The second deluge was one too many. It emptied out the West Otago township. Well, almost.

I remember Kelso from a visit in the 1970s. Driving through the rolling sheep and cattle country planning a Heartland column in 2012, I have trouble finding the town. Just as I am wondering how a town can disappear without trace, the road tops a hill and rounds a bend and ahead of me on the downward slope stand the gaunt concrete walls of the former dairy factory. Now I know where I am. I continue down the hill to where the town used to be. There I find some traces of old Kelso. The embankment where the Heriot branch railway used to run can still be seen. A faded red railway goods shed stands beside it.

Near the railway shed is a large billboard explaining the town's fate. Floods in 1978 and 1980 are both labelled "100-year" events. Each flood occurred when raging waters of the Pomahaka River, on one side of Kelso, and

Crookston Burn (love the Scottishness of it!) on the other side surged together after heavy rain to create a plunging, bucking wall of water two metres deep that engulfed the township. That was the 1978 flood. The 1980 wall of water was even higher. The waters were 60 centimetres higher. Helicopters plucked people off rooftops as waters lapped at the spouting.

After the first event, locals returned to their homes and cleaned up the mess. A flood relief fund offered finance to help residents get back to normal but these stout folk declined to accept help.

They didn't decline after the next flood, though. Nearly all of the 150 permanent residents decided to move away. The fund helped them shift buildings and become re-established in other towns. Joining the exodus were two stores, a garage, a stock and station firm, a church, a school, a hall and the rugby clubrooms. No wonder I have difficulty finding the place.

Of this quintessential New Zealand farming village only four buildings remain standing – three houses and the shelter sheds of the

Opposite: Floods in 1978 and 1980 wiped out the West Otago town of Kelso. The railway goods shed is one of few buildings remaining after the town was evacuated. A memorial and information board show visitors the extent of the flood damage.

former school, all on slightly elevated ground. Beside the school I see the remains of the swimming baths.

No one answers my knock at two of the houses but at the third I meet Russell Dynes. He is the last of the Kelsonians. He tells me only two other families stayed after 1980 and they have since left. But he has lived all his life here and will never move. He has raised his house on high piles and will "stick it out".

Semi-retired and in his mid-60s, Dynes drives the daily school bus taking farm children to and from Heriot Primary School and high school students to and from Tapanui's Blue Mountain College.

It is impossible to calculate the odds of another "100-year" flood in Dynes' lifetime. He merely shrugs at the thought. It is impossible, too, to put a price on the contentment he feels at being in his own home.

I wonder if those who left Kelso are pining now for this idyllic valley where two rivers twice joined hands to deliver trauma and despair.

TRAUMA – WHAT COULD BE more traumatic than an armed man going berserk in a peaceful place and shooting innocent people dead? Three examples in lonely South Island locations still convey a sense of horror.

West Coast loner Stanley Graham sparked New Zealand's most famous manhunt early in World War II. Personal and financial problems had been dogging the Kowhitirangi farmer when he began his murderous rampage. He then packed his rifle and took to the hills. Police and military forces tracked him in dense bush. Eventually he was found and shot. He died in hospital from his wounds. His house was then burned down, "mysteriously" they say.

Kowhitirangi and its near neighbour Kokatahi sit in one of the most beautiful parts of the West Coast. A wide valley of lushest green is backed by steep hills clad in bush that rear up to snow-garbed alps. The Hokitika River rollicks through its narrow gorge at the foot of the hills and rolls across the plain, to reach the Tasman Sea 20 kilometres away at Hokitika town.

Kokatahi enjoys its fame as the home of an unusual musical band that achieved national popularity in the 1970s. Kowhitirangi is a little more subdued about its fame as the home of a mass killer. Nevertheless, when I visit in 2007, local farmers at a working bee do not seem to mind talking about it to help me with a Heartland column.

The working bee is a Kowhitirangi Community Society project to turn the recently closed school into a camping ground and holiday park. After we have chatted for a while, I ask where Graham's house stood.

"Right behind you, over the road," one man says.

I cross over and find a monument to the seven victims, on the spot where Graham's house burned to the ground. I reflect there for a minute

Opposite: Aramoana, pathway to the sea: Gunshots shattered the silence of the seaside settlement near the ocean end of Otago Harbour in late 1990. Resident David Gray shot and killed 13 others, including a police officer, before he too was shot, by another police officer.

on how tortured Graham must have been in his mind, of how horrified valley residents must have felt as those events unfolded in 1941. Then I gaze at the wider scene. It seems like paradise. I wonder at the incongruity of such dark deeds in such a magnificent setting.

A different community dwells at Aramoana. A different response to my visit there reflects the residents' distaste for strangers snooping around the killing fields where David Gray murdered 12 people and where he was then slain in 1990.

I drive out from Dunedin in 2006, skirting Otago Harbour, past Port Chalmers, to the end of the road. This is Aramoana, "pathway to the sea", home to lovers of nature.

Residents live in add-on shacks, crude cribs, clapped-out buses and some nice houses. Around them are scrubby sand dunes and wind-withered trees. The harshness of the environment is their bulwark against property developers. Demand for homes here is slack. The locals roused themselves once, to defeat a proposed aluminium smelter here in the 1970s. They were roused again by the gunshots of 1990.

The few people I see turn their backs and shuffle away before I can ask them where the memorial to the victims of Gray's gun stands. So I go looking in the sandhills and find the modernist tribute, strangely hidden in a hollow. As at Kowhitirangi, I sense the incongruity of mass murders in this peaceful spot.

Later I get chatting to long-time resident Lina Davis. She refers to the 1990 incident as "the massacre". She admits the locals are "getting a bit vexed" with nosy visitors asking about David Gray and the whereabouts of his house. Residents may talk about it among themselves but not with strangers, she says.

A movie about the massacre was made, called *Out of the Blue*. It stirred up interest anew. From that point Davis has tended to stay indoors at weekends to avoid the voyeurs who drive down to Aramoana. I drive away feeling chastened.

In a corner of the Nelson Lakes district, up a back road near Lake Rotoiti, stands the historic Tophouse Hotel. And there the incongruity continues. For, in this tranquil and beautiful mountain place yet another man raised his gun and fired, killing two innocent victims and then himself.

Stanley Graham and David Gray were tortured personalities. Bill Bateman was a simple lad driven to a frenzy by jealousy and the teasing of fellow farmhands.

Hotel lessee Jennifer Sloots knows the details off by heart. In this lonely spot, a hotel needs a point of difference to attract customers. For Tophouse, tragedy is it. When I pop in there in 2012, Sloots leads me to the veranda post where Bateman's body was found, slumped and dead. She points out the gunshot holes in the veranda roof. Then she tells me the story.

The story certainly attracts visitors. The day I call, 11 people are lunching in the hotel dining room. Former owner Nigel Phoenix once told me the macabre setting was a popular choice for visitors to take their Devonshire teas.

Bateman was "not mad, just madly in love", says Sloots. The object of his affections was Catherine Wylie, who worked as governess for the owner's children in the days when Tophouse was a staging post for coach services, being roughly equidistant from Blenheim, Nelson and Murchison. The owner and his wife went away for a break, leaving Wylie in charge of the children and asking John Lane to run the business. Bateman regarded Lane as his rival for Wylie's hand.

After a boozing binge, in which other young men of the district had teased him about Wylie and Lane, Bateman borrowed the postmaster's shotgun, lured Lane outside on the pretext of going to shoot hares together, and blew him to bits. Then, seeking to cover his traces, Bateman lured the postmaster outside and blasted him too.

Bateman then returned to the hotel and asked Wylie to join him in some hare shooting. Perhaps from the sound of shots, perhaps from the look on Bateman's face, Wylie sensed something was up. To buy time she said she would come out after she had put the children to bed. Then she slipped out to the telegraph office and sent a cable to police in Nelson.

When Bateman realised Wylie was at the telegraph office, he cut the wires. It was too late – the message had gone. He realised "the game was up". He returned to swigging from a bottle of whisky on the pub veranda.

A quick search by police next day found the bodies of Bateman's victims. Both had been shot in the head. Bateman had then made cursory attempts to hide them, one in a wood pile, the other under a horse blanket.

The position of Bateman's own corpse indicated he had placed the gun between his legs with the barrel in his mouth. He had pushed the trigger with his bare toe. An empty whisky bottle lay beside him.

Left: A country pub needs a point of difference to attract passers-by. Tophouse Hotel, near St Arnaud in northern Nelson, has one. Lessee Jennifer Sloots, (left) and staff member Katie Burke show the spot where double murderer Bill Bateman shot himself for the unrequited love of a woman in 1894.
Mike Crean Fairfax Media NZ/ The Press

Leaving Tophouse, I drive through the mountain village of St Arnaud and the incongruity of murder and scenic magnificence strikes me even more strongly. For St Arnaud is a place of healing, not killing. In a grove of native bush where birds sing louder than guns, a series of alpine-style cottages provides respite for people suffering from domestic violence. Amid the cottages stands a chapel, its large window providing a panoramic view of lovely Lake Rotoiti.

The cottages and chapel were the bequest of Nelson policeman Noel Oxnam. His work had too often involved dealing with dysfunctional families and abusive relationships. He saw the need for a haven where the troubled and the hurt could find solace. He drove fundraising to bring his vision to reality in the 1980s.

Above: Deranged West Coaster farmer Stanley Graham ran amok with a rifle killing seven people in 1941. A large manhunt tracked him down. He was shot and died in hospital. Residents of Kowhitirangi erected this monument to victims of the shootings on the site of Graham's burned-down house.

Below: One year after David Gray's massacre of 13 Aramoana residents, the small seaside community unveiled this monument to the victims in a hollow among the sandhills, beside Otago Harbour.

Right: This 1948 train disaster at Blind River, near Seddon in Marlborough, was tragically similar to the Hyde disaster. This Christchurch-bound train was carrying 150 passengers when it took a bend too fast and crashed. Six people were killed and 37 admitted to hospital with injuries.
Marlborough Historical Society

Opposite: The scene of the Blind River crash in 2015. The Cook Strait ferry service has boosted freight volumes on the railway but air travel and increased car ownership have slashed train passenger numbers.

RAILWAYS BROUGHT NEW ZEALAND'S far-flung localities together in the 1800s. They also brought disasters. The biggest was at Tangiwai, in the North Island, in 1953. The South Island has had major train disasters too. A fatal crash at Blind River, in Marlborough, pre-dated Tangiwai by five years.

Young Seddon farmhand Trevor Marfell was releasing his horse team from harness for a lunch break one February day in 1948. Suddenly he heard the Picton to Christchurch express screeching as it took a bend too fast. Then came the thunderous cacophony of sounds he would never forget as the train rocketed off the rails and into the side of a cutting.

Marfell, a fit rugby player, raced to his boss's house and raised the alarm. The rest remained "a bit of a blur" he tells me in 2013, as he tries to remember the crash.

He recalls the train's guard reaching the house, sweating and heaving for breath and collapsing at the front door. He remembers a line of ambulances arriving later to take the 37 injured passengers to hospital in Blenheim. Then a Seddon transport truck carted away six lifeless bodies, covered by a tarpaulin.

Marfell's aunt, Eva Smith, was a survivor of the crash. She had boarded the train at Seddon, 20 kilometres south of Blenheim. She later told Marfell how she had barely got comfortable in her seat when the train began to rock and lurch at a bend just before Blind River. The violence of the train's gyrations shocked the 150 passengers. Some reached for the emergency stop lever. But only the bank could stop this train.

If you take a loop road eastward off State Highway 1 between Seddon and Ward, you will wind through parched hills where the only greenness is in grape vines. Soon the road crosses the main trunk line. Near the crossing you can just see where the small Blind River railway station once stood. Children attended a one-teacher school nearby but it has long closed. Blind River never amounted to much more.

Farmers in this coastal hill area of Marlborough have always struggled with drought. The train disaster brought the area some brief but unwanted prominence.

I ask some folk at Ward how Blind River got its name and they can only shrug. They seem to take the name for granted. However, Kevin Brooker has an answer. He says the

stream "just seems to stop – it is blind". So I follow the stream through the low hills. Sure enough, I soon come to a spot, just east of the loop road bridge, where the water seems to disappear underground.

The Blind River train crash sparked court proceedings. The driver admitted exceeding the speed limit for that section of track and was charged with manslaughter. However, he was acquitted and the blame was laid with New Zealand Railways. The driver was inexperienced and should not have been assigned to drive the express, the court found. To make matters worse, the locomotive had not been fitted with a speedometer, so a driver would have had to gauge the train's speed from experience.

Six people dead, 37 seriously injured – it must have seemed that Railways had failed to learn a lesson. For the Blind River crash came only five years after a hauntingly similar disaster had occurred. The Hyde train crash in 1943 was New Zealand's worst before Tangiwai.

Twenty-one people were killed at Hyde, near Ranfurly, in the shade of Otago's rugged Rock and Pillar Range. On a cold but clear Queen's Birthday Friday their packed passenger train, travelling from Cromwell to Dunedin, took a bend too fast. It jolted off the rails and slammed into a high bank.

Disaster it was but highly publicised it was not. World War II was raging and the news was dominated by events from the battle fronts. Also, public morale was important for the war effort. Reports of disasters, if not hushed up, were at least subdued.

I first heard of the Hyde disaster when reading of Southland woman Elizabeth Coleman's proposal in 1990 for a monument to the victims to mark the 50th anniversary.

Response to the proposal was positive and the monument now stands beside the Middlemarch-Ranfurly road, a short walk from the cutting. I visited the site, on Gerald Kinney's

farm, later in 1990. Kinney's interest in the crash was twofold. Not only did the railway run through his family's farm, but his older brother, Frank, was a victim of the crash.

Gerald explains that Frank boarded the train about 3.15pm at the little Hyde station, bound for Dunedin and the annual Winter Show. Gerald, then 16, had been working at the back of the farm that day and knew nothing of the crash until he rode his horse into the yard and heard the news.

The boys' father had watched the train pass as he was moving sheep in a paddock near the tracks. Even as he waved at the blur of faces in the carriages, he sensed something was wrong. He had heard trains go past hundreds of times and this one did not sound right. It was going too fast. At the next sound, his stomach lurched. It was the hellish noise of iron shattering against rock and the locomotive's boiler bursting as the train plummeted into the wall of a cutting.

Gerald takes me down the paddock to the cutting. Even after 47 years, bits of rusty iron still lie in spindly grass beside the track and embedded in earth halfway up the bank. Until Elizabeth Coleman came along, this twisted metal mess was the victims' only memorial.

Gerald Kinney lost a brother here. Elizabeth Coleman lost her father and a brother.

Doctors from around the district converged on the scene. In an account for the Middlemarch Museum, Dr Adrian Webb described the nightmare he found in the cutting that day – the locomotive stoker badly scalded by water from the burst boiler, the driver severely injured after having been thrown from the cab by the impact.

Crawling into a "mass of splintered wood, bent steel, broken seats and doors", Webb found a young woman pinned under a part of the under-carriage. A fellow doctor said they would have to amputate her legs to get her out.

Webb disagreed and called for help from a railways work gang that had just arrived. They used an oxy-acetylene cutter and a jack to remove the weight from the passenger, and her legs were saved.

Bodies of the 21 victims were laid out beside the road and covered with coats and rugs. Hearing of the tragedy, family and friends arrived to identify the dead. Then they stood, numbed by the gathering cold and the awful emptiness in their hearts. About 8pm some buses arrived from Dunedin and the scene emptied of people.

As with Blind River, court action followed. But this time the driver, John Corcoran, was convicted of manslaughter. He appeared in the dock, mostly recovered from his physical injuries but stricken with remorse. The court heard he had been drinking shortly before the crash, while the train was taking a refreshments stop at Ranfurly. He served a term of imprisonment and died not long after.

Two railway disasters in five years. Add the Tangiwai disaster and it's three in 10 years. Rail was a common mode of travel in those times. Perhaps its toll should be compared with numbers of road deaths in the modern age.

Below: New Zealand's worst train crash, at the time, cost 21 lives. Excessive speed on a bend caused this train, bound for Dunedin in 1943, to run off the rails and slam into the side of the cutting near Hyde in the Maniototo district.
Otago Daily Times

This monument to the 21 victims stands beside the Middlemarch-Ranfurly road, near the cutting where the speeding train left the rails and crashed.

Speak of South Island disasters and most people's minds will turn to earthquakes. With the Canterbury quakes of 2010 and 2011 still stirring my emotions, I bump down to Brooklands. "Bump" because the roads to, and in, this forgotten north-eastern corner of Christchurch are badly damaged.

Down there the leafy branches of English trees droop into the languid waters of the Styx River above its confluence with the Waimakariri. The Brooklands Lagoon acts like a moat to separate houses from sandhills within earshot of the Pacific surf pounding.

But what houses? The sight that meets me could be from a war scene after the bombing and shelling has stopped and the troops have moved on. Where families once lived and played, demolition crews have left rows and rows of ugly gaps between the few remaining houses that lean forlorn, buckled and broken, their owners seeming damned to eternal argument with the Earthquake Commission and insurance companies.

I recall the old Brooklands – a rural community of small farms where the sluggish motion of cows set the tone for residents, a friendly community that enjoyed dances, parties and weddings in the village hall, a welcoming community where city slickers drove on Sundays for peace and picnics and ice creams at the shop.

That changed when Brooklands became absorbed into the expanded Christchurch City as part of local government restructuring in the 1980s. The change brought promises of sewers and other services. The promises brought property developers who slapped up houses for newcomers who wanted to escape the city's rush areas and savour the sea air.

Those changes were as nothing compared to the tremors of February 2011, and the aftershocks that persisted for months thereafter. No one was killed at Brooklands by the earthquakes but the village itself died. Well, almost. Some residents, united in a bond of determination and love for the place, have defied all authority and stayed.

Earthquakes were more commonly associated with the Buller and Nelson areas. The magnitude 7.1 Inangahua earthquake of 1968 left three people dead. It left many more scarred. It caused landslides that scoured the hills around the point where the Inangahua River flows into the Buller River. A massive slip dammed the Buller, raising fears of a deluge if the dam broke suddenly and released its waters through the river's lower gorge, from which they might rush all the way to Westport.

Stopping at the tiny Inangahua Village township in 2006, I chat with some locals. For dairy farmers Liza and Peter van Lugt, the memories of terror and bewilderment are still fresh nearly 40 years after the big shake. They describe how a helicopter landed at their place and an official ordered them to leave because of the flood threat. Fearing newly opened craters in the road might swallow whole cars, they picked their way on foot to join other fleeing residents at The Landing.

Left: The ground under them shifted violently and was declared unfit to live on. Many Brooklands residents moved away but the stubborn ones stayed. The beachside settlement on the north-east edge of Christchurch had been their paradise before the earthquakes of February, 2011. They believed it would be again, in spite of damage to buildings and roads and the loss of services.

Families forced from their homes gathered here, eight kilometres up the Inangahua River, where supply boats used to tie up after their long beat upstream from Westport. Generous Reefton folk drove down to The Landing and took shocked victims of the quake to their homes 30 kilometres away.

Liza and her children were billeted at Reefton for three months while Peter returned to the farm to tend the cows. The house had lost its chimneys and many contents were broken. Aftershocks and landslides continued, so road repairs were impossible. Peter did not get his car out of the garage for seven weeks.

Amid the hardships, one good memory persists. The people rallied round and helped one another. Community spirit was marvellous, Peter says.

Many other disasters have afflicted South Islanders. Coal mining tragedies have taken a terrible toll in human life. A monument at Kaitangata, near Balclutha in South Otago, commemorates the 34 victims of a gas explosion down the mine in 1879. This was one of New Zealand's earliest and worst mine disasters.

One of the latest (and among the worst) was at Pike River, near Greymouth, in 2010. On a West Coast road trip five years later I hear Cobden people say they are still grieving for the Pike River victims. Several of the 29 men who were killed were Cobden residents.

"Everyone knew someone who was down that mine," one woman tells me.

That's the nature of the South Island. It is small enough for many people to know of someone who was killed in a disaster.

Below: The whole nation mourned and every West Coaster knew someone among the 29 coal miners killed in the 2010 Pike River tragedy. The men's bodies were, controversially, never recovered. As the mine is their tomb, this memorial in the hills north of Greymouth is their headstone.

CHAPTER 3

From rails to trails

Driving from Christchurch to Kaikoura, you cross the Conway River and thread your way through the Hundalee Hills, before plunging down to the sea at Oaro. There, on your right, is a Maori village. On your left, well, there is not much now but once this was the site of an expansive railway town.

The last link in building the South Island Main Trunk railway line was the most difficult. Precipitous mountain slopes soar above a rocky coastline where the Pacific Ocean belies its name by roaring and raging against the land in frequent high winds. The terrain is not just difficult, it keeps shifting. Landslips occasionally smother road and railway after heavy rains.

The challenge of laying iron tracks along the coast from Claverley to Peketa seemed too great at first. So completion of the main trunk stalled at Parnassus for nearly 30 years while engineers, officials and politicians dithered over the route to take. A start was made on pushing the tracks inland up the Leader Valley. Look to your left just north of Parnassus, before you cross the Leader River, and you can see the embankment that was built for this purpose. A little way up the Leader Road concrete abutments for a railway bridge can still be seen.

While all this was going on, Parnassus was the terminus of the main trunk going north from Christchurch. Passengers arriving by train transferred to coaches there for the tortuous road trip to Kaikoura.

Parnassus farmer Paul Bush remembers the trains coming up from Christchurch in the 1930s. As a youngster he watched as locomotives were swung around on a turntable near the busy station and then, smoke and steam billowing, dragged their trains back south. He recalls railway stockyards frequently packed with sheep and cattle from local stations, destined for the Addington market and the various freezing works around Christchurch. The stationmaster was also the postmaster in what was virtually a railways town, Bush says.

At long last, the decision was made to tackle the seaward route, down the Conway to Claverley and along the coast. Oaro became a major settlement for the workers on this project. They completed the job, and the final link in the main trunk, as late as 1945.

Train passengers today would barely notice Parnassus as they glide through. Neither would they recognise anything of Claverley's

Opposite: The north-bound Coastal Pacific train rushes disdainfully past a railway pioneer on the South Island Main Trunk at Oaro, south of Kaikoura. The rusty, old steam locomotive was dumped beside the line to help strengthen the sea wall in an area where land slips and tidal erosion pose problems for the railway.

stormy past. A Maori pa stood at Claverley for two centuries from the 1600s. The story goes that a visiting Ngai Tahu party arrived there to negotiate a marriage. The nuptial arrangements never got started, as the resident Maori locked up the visitors then massacred them as revenge for a previous killing. One Ngai Tahu warrior managed to escape, but only by climbing the palisade, sprinting to the cliff overlooking the sea and jumping into space. Luckily he landed in soft sand and got away.

Little can be seen of this historic site today. Claverley in the 1930s became another railway builders' camp. Men from here dug out part of the Haumuri Bluffs Tunnel, the second-longest in the South Island Main Trunk at nearly one kilometre.

I chat to two women at Oaro in 2011. One is from the Maori village on the site of another old pa. The other lives in one of the few remaining houses in the European settlement. They modestly ask not to be named as they reminisce on Oaro in its days as a railway town.

There was a hierarchy, they say. Single men lived in huts on the east side of the tracks, while their bosses resided in substantial homes on the elevated western side. Maori and European residents mingled at the three-teacher school, in the store and Post Office and at

the swimming hole in a small lagoon of the Oaro River. Few people had cars so shopping trips were made by train to Kaikoura or Christchurch once the railway line was opened.

The women recommend I take the walkway beside the railway to the mouth of the Haumuri Bluffs Tunnel. The walkway serves also as an access road for railway maintenance crews. They advise me to bypass the Maori village by taking the track down to the beach and onto the trail. However, as I reach the track a Maori man in the village calls out to me and we have a chat. He insists it is fine for me to go through the village, so I do.

Among the relics on this 90-minute return walk is a rusted old steam locomotive that was tipped over the edge of the railway bank to form part of the seawall. I also find the overgrown entrance to another railway tunnel. The tunnel was abandoned when earthquakes caused its walls to buckle. The track was diverted around a spur to sit giddily above the breaking surf.

That's the same moving earth that made the whole Kaikoura Coast so troublesome to road and rail building gangs.

As the spread of railways opened up rural areas, other towns also provided homes for track builders and maintenance gangs. Springfield, in Central Canterbury, blossomed with

construction of the Midland Line from Christchurch to Greymouth through the Southern Alps.

Springfield is the point where travellers to the West Coast leave the Canterbury Plains behind and plunge into the alpine foothills. Farmer Murray Wason tells me Springfield became virtually two towns in the great railways era. Mining of coal and excavation of clay for local brick works, as well as farming, spawned the original settlement. When the Arthurs Pass-Otira route was chosen for the railway, a second settlement sprang up at the western edge of Springfield. Wason points out the few remaining houses of the 22 that once accommodated the railwaymen and their families there. This precinct became known as White City, as all the houses were painted white, he says.

A few more relics of railway workers and their families can be seen at Kowai Flat, another railway town just "a stone's throw" up the track from Springfield. Further up the line again is Cass, where 500 railway people once lived. Only one railway house is still in use there. The former station at Cass was immortalised in a Rita Angus painting that was voted New Zealand's most popular art work in a *Listener* magazine feature.

At Cass in 2009, I meet grader driver Dusty Cornelius, who has stopped to eat his lunch. I ask if he will pose for a photograph and he agrees. I explain that I want the image to show the same scene as the Angus painting. Angus sat a male figure on the station platform, which no longer exists, so I get Cornelius to squat where the platform once was. Then, looking at the background, some of it obscured by a belt of pine trees, I start to realise how much artistic licence Angus took with the landscape.

My photo would win no prize but the idea must have been a good one as TV3 News copied the concept a couple of weeks later.

Above: The railway town at Cass has gone but the trains keep coming. These days nearly all the trains are carrying coal from Buller to Lyttelton for export. Cass, named after an early Canterbury surveyor, is on the Midland Line, east of Arthurs Pass.

Opposite: The former State Highway 1 passes the former Parnassus store. Discuss Parnassus and you find the word former keeps popping into the conversation. The sleepy hollow, bypassed by a sweeping new highway, was formerly a busy railway and bus terminus – until the section of Main Trunk railway to Kaikoura was completed in the 1940s.

Right: A high proportion of travellers driving through the Southern Alps stop at Arthurs Pass village. And why not? With mountain grandeur all around, good eating places, comical kea (native parrots) welcoming you and, since this is still east of the Main Divide, mostly fine weather.

Arthurs Pass and Otira villages boomed for the building of the Otira Tunnel, New Zealand's longest. They continued to prosper while electric locomotives were housed and maintained for many years to drag trains through the tunnel, where smoke from steam locomotives would have been suffocating. A few quaint railway cottages still stand beside the road through Arthurs Pass. The workers' leisure rooms are now an outdoor education camp for visiting school groups. Former railway houses at Otira look like boats adrift in a sea of dilapidation.

Oaro, Parnassus, Springfield, Kowai Flat, Cass, Arthurs Pass, Otira – railway towns all. And there are many more around the South Island. Railway buildings tend to look similar, as if they are wearing a compulsory uniform. But the people who lived and worked in them were as diverse as in any community. One thing they had in common, though. They were tough. They had to be, because railway building was hard slog, often at the very frontier of New Zealand life.

Among the people hardy enough to take it on was a force of Polish immigrants at Lake Waihola, south of Dunedin.

Placid Lake Waihola was once a venue for rowing regattas. But its waters seldom remain placid for long and it has been little used since Twizel's lake Ruataniwha was created. I pop into the Waihola District School in 2014 to chat with the principal, Sara Whitaker. She outlines a history project which the pupils

Right: Otira – where the mountains close in under tragedian clouds, where the road begins its tortuous climb to Arthurs Pass, where the railway disappears into New Zealand's longest tunnel. Otira – where you depart the West Coast and plunge into wilderness.

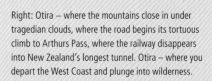

Left: The placid waters of Lake Waihola, south of Dunedin, suit anglers and oarsmen. However, they seldom stay placid for long. Winds build up waves which often make the lake too choppy for rowing, so many competitive events have moved to Lake Ruataniwha, in the Mackenzie Country.

have done, involving interviews with long-time residents. One of their findings is that Polish immigrants were prominent early settlers here. The men worked on building the Main Trunk line from the south end of the Taieri Plain to the town of Milton. Suddenly it made sense to the children that one of them had a Polish surname, Whitaker says.

I look for Polish names on headstones in the Lake Waihola cemetery but can see only one. The headstone stands at the grave of the Baumgardt family. Why only one? Local resident Jean Timms, who helped the pupils with their history project, explains that many of the Poles anglicised their names. Even the Baumgardts changed theirs – to Bungard.

What pressures could have driven these hard-working Poles to conceal their past? Unfortunately there are no descendants left for me to ask. When people like Jean Timms pass on, who then will tell of such snippets as the cherry plum trees the Poles planted at Lake Waihola to make their favourite brew, cherry brandy?

You might say Otago's Lake Waihola and Southland's Round Hill are poles apart. For it was Chinese workers, not Polish, who worked on a section of the railway from Invercargill, westwards along the southern coast of Southland. At Round Hill, in bush country north-west of Riverton, they established New Zealand's biggest Chinatown. In the 1870s and 1880s it was thought to be the most southern Chinese settlement in the world.

Carole Power of Te Hikoi Southern Encounter museum at Riverton says the Chinese came to the district as gold miners after European diggers abandoned the field from 1871. At first the Chinese dug over the old workings but with declining success. Then a sluicing company moved in and water races were needed to bring water from 40 kilometres away. Many of the Chinese had experience of digging water races for the paddy fields of home. They "had an eye" for calculating levels around hillsides and did an excellent job for the sluicing company, Power says.

When that project was completed, the Chinese found another task that suited their talent. The railway was being pushed west, past Riverton and on to Tuatapere. The route skirted many hills so workers who could "read" the contours of the land and build gradual gradients to suit trains were needed. The Chinese excelled again in this work. When that job was finished, most of them moved away. It is difficult today to find any trace of their southernmost Chinatown.

The Tuatapere line has long since closed. In this it is typical of most South Island branch lines. However, closed they may be but the keen eye can detect clues to their historic whereabouts in many parts of the countryside, reflecting railways' profligate spread: West Eyreton near Rangiora, Waiau in North Canterbury, Glenhope south of Nelson, Ross in Westland, Tahakopa in The Catlins, Heriot north of Gore, Roxburgh in Central Otago, Ngapara and Duntroon in North Otago, Fairlie in South Canterbury, Mt Somers in Mid Canterbury, Oxford-Sheffield in Canterbury, and more.

Research and interviews with locals for my South Island trips unearthed some good stories about railways. Many stories involve hotels. In town after town you will still find a Railway Hotel, though no railway has run there for half a century. Hotels were commonly erected near railway stations to offer accommodation to travellers stopping overnight. Waikari, in North Canterbury, had two pubs handy to the tracks, the Great Northern and the Star and Garter.

The Waikari Hill, leading out of the town and into the Weka Pass, was the steepest climb on the Waiau branch line. It was on this line, at Culverden, that the fabled Molesworth cattle drives ended each year. Molesworth, New Zealand's biggest sheep and cattle station, covers 181,000 mountainous hectares in central Marlborough. Stock mustered and driven overland for days on end by cowboys on horses attracted an army of spectators, many shooting movie film and still photographs of this "Wild West" event.

Right: Vintage trains run excursions on the Weka Pass Railway, in North Canterbury. The section of line from Waipara to Waikari survived the closure of the Waiau branch line nearly 40 years ago. Volunteers continue to maintain it so steam locomotives can be seen billowing coal smoke as they pound through the gap behind Frog Rock.

The cattle were loaded onto special trains at the Culverden railway station, their destination the Addington saleyards in Christchurch.

Trains hauling livestock, logs, wool and grain would stop briefly at the Waikari station on their way south. Departing from there, they would almost immediately confront the Waikari Hill. On a winter's evening the tracks could be slippery with frost. Bar patrons at the two local pubs would place bets on how many attempts the driver would have to make before his train would conquer the summit and disappear into the night.

Once, twice, even three times, the train might grind to a halt on the hill. The driver would reverse it some two kilometres down the line, beyond the station, as far as the Waikari flour mill. Then, with full steam up, he would launch another tilt at the hill. Rousing cheers would fill the hotel's bars at each assault.

The drinkers were breaking the liquor law of six-o'clock closing in those days. They might have been in breach of the gambling laws as well. The publicans, fearing the local constable might hear, would try to hush them. Their efforts had little success.

The Waiau branch line closed in 1978 after taking away the last loads of logs from trees blown over in the 1975 gales at Balmoral Forest, near Culverden. The section of track from Waipara to Waikari, including the Weka Pass, has been retained. Weka Pass excursion trains now carry delighted passengers on this track. The terminus is halfway down the Waikari Hill. Passengers alighting there may be tempted by the Star and Garter Hotel just a few metres below them. Its rival, the Great Northern, burned down in 2013.

Liquor was a common theme in other stories. Mandeville, on the Waimea Plain branch line just west of Gore, and Chertsey on the main trunk line just north of Ashburton, profited from prohibition in the 1950s. Gore and Ashburton were both "dry" towns, Mandeville and Chertsey were "wet", in the days when voters could choose the prohibition of liquor sales in their electorates.

Would-be drinkers in Gore and Ashburton became frequent users of the railway. Not many trains ran on the Waimea line, from Gore to Lumsden, so the thirsty sometimes had to make the 20 kilometre pilgrimage to Mandeville by bike. This made them even thirstier, so they could not be blamed for waiting for a train to take them home much later. If it was a goods train, they would ask the guard if they could stash their bikes in the guard's van. Guards being accommodating chaps, refusals were rare. According to local Maeva Smith, the Mandeville Hotel did a roaring trade in those days. Now it is a cafe.

Mandeville is known today for its aircraft restoration workshop and classic aircraft museum. The little township is sheltered from wind and rain by the legendary Hokonui Hills. I enjoy the irony of drinkers going to great lengths for a tipple in the bar there, so close to the rugged Hokonui gullies where once the smoke coiling upwards from fires in bush huts indicated the activities of illicit whisky distillers.

Gore's Hokonui Heritage Museum heritage curator Jim Geddes tells me about pioneering distiller Mary McRae. The Scottish Highlands widow arrived in the district in 1872 with her seven children and a box labelled "household goods". The household goods were actually the paraphernalia for distilling whisky. She had heard that imported Scotch whisky was being diluted by thieves on the wharves in antipodean ports. The cunning crooks would tap part of a barrel and refill it with water.

This was no good for McRae. She wanted "the real stuff", Geddes says.

McRae and her family produced full-strength "hootch" high in the Hokonui Hills and delivered it to safe houses in several towns, where regular buyers could collect it. The Catholic presbytery (priest's house) in Balclutha was one such depot, Geddes said. McRae always sent a bottle to the local police chief and judge as well – as a sort of insurance policy.

Above: Julie Blackler of the Hokonui Moonshine Museum at Gore explains the working of an illicit whisky distillery modelled on those used in the Hokonui Hills during the liquor prohibition era.

Opposite: Much of Southland "went dry" a century ago, when electors voted for prohibition. Hardened drinkers from Gore then took the Lumsden train, or pedalled their bikes, to enjoy a few beers at the Mandeville Hotel, 20 kilometres out of town. The pub has been remodelled as a cafe, next to Mandeville's chief attraction – an aircraft museum and restoration workshop.

Below: The Chertsey Hotel is a stone's throw from the railway tracks, which proved very convenient for Ashburton tipplers in prohibition days. Train timetables enabled drinkers in "dry" Ashburton to hitch a ride north after work, guzzle a few glasses in this liquor oasis, and catch another train home again.

Illegal distilling increased during the 1930s depression and again during prohibition in the 1950s. It was not all made in the Hokonui Hills but Hokonui became a generic name for much of it, Geddes says.

The railway provided a service to Ashburton drinkers, though management may not have been aware of it. The daily Invercargill to Christchurch passenger train was scheduled to get inter-island passengers to the wharf at Lyttelton in time to board the overnight ferry to Wellington. It stopped briefly at Ashburton at a time that was convenient to workers just knocking off from a day's toil. A quarter of an hour down the line, they would step down from the train and cross the road to the Chertsey Hotel. Chertsey publican Dianne Smith says some workers who missed the train would bike to the pub, often into a Canterbury nor'wester.

When they were ready to return to their homes, the night train from Christchurch to Invercargill would be due. Again, very convenient. And for anyone who missed out, the Chertsey Hotel ran a black market in booze. Smith is not sure if the contraband liquor was carried by rail to Ashburton. That might have been just too convenient. Perhaps the publican carted it himself.

It is said that seldom, if ever, did the Ashburton drinkers have to pay for their ride. They knew from which end of the train the guard would start checking passengers' tickets. They would be gone before he reached their carriage.

Perhaps this was a reflection of solidarity among railway people. The railway maintenance staff at Parnassus had no access to a pub, so the local garage proprietor used to order a keg of beer from a brewery in Christchurch for them each Friday. This was brought up on the train at a "very favourable rate".

You might expect a story about people sitting on the railway tracks would have something to do with booze, too. But the 10 women who sat on the rails, knitting and sewing, at the isolated Kiwi station, in rural Nelson, were very sober. Among them was a young Sonja Davies. She would achieve prominence later in life as an MP and activist for peace and women's rights.

The women were protesting at the closing of the Nelson line, demolition of railway buildings and the lifting of the rails so the line could not be re-opened. They had previously blocked demolition of the railway goods shed by taking up occupation in it. They staged their sit-down protest as the demolition train was approaching.

Left: "Don't rip up our railway!" This was the message of protest leader Ruth Page and other women when police arrested them in 1955. The Government's decision to close the Nelson railway was unpopular and the women's protest gained widespread support. The scene is the isolated Kiwi Station where the demolition train was approaching.
Nelson Provincial Museum

The Kiwi railway station was in the news when women protesting against closure of the Nelson Railway in 1955 were arrested. The women lost their cause but the little building was saved. Shifted to Tapawera, it speaks proudly of an event that galvanised the Nelson region.

Opposition to the closure of the line was widespread and strong. The women appeared in court and were found guilty of trespassing on railway property and obstructing railway work. Fines were imposed but the community took up a collection which raised enough money to pay them. To further enhance the reputation of railway guards, the guard on the demolition train at Kiwi walked off the job in sympathy with the women protesters. He became a local hero.

Yes, Nelson did have a railway. It is an epic story and too long to tell here. Enough to say the 100 kilometres of track from Nelson City to lonely Kawatiri Junction, north of Murchison, took 80 years to build. It was planned to link with the West Coast line at Inangahua Junction. Instead, it was quickly shortened to a terminus at Glenhope and closed not long after, in 1955.

No trains pass through Kiwi now. The day I drive there, half a century later, the road from Glenhope is narrow, winding, rutted and dusty. I suspect few cars pass through there either.

In more recent times, the closure of railway lines has led to new and positive ventures. Even the vexed story of the Nelson line has a happy ending. Sections of the track, and the tunnel from Belgrove to Tapawera, are being incorporated into cycle trails.

The Otago Central line, from Wingatui (in Mosgiel) to Cromwell was kept open as far as Clyde to transport materials for the Clyde Dam construction in the late 1970s. The Clyde to Cromwell section was then flooded by the newly created lake.

The Wingatui-Middlemarch section of the line was retained for the Taieri Gorge excursion train service. The rest of the tracks were lifted. Thoughts then turned to possible uses of this vacant "rail corridor" through part of Central Otago. Cycling interests called for a walking, cycling and horse riding trail. Farmers along the line objected but, once the trail was opened, many changed their tune. With farming in the economic doldrums, the opportunities that the rail trail offered for making

Right: Viaducts and tunnels on the former Otago Central railway corridor add excitement for riders on the rail trail. The trail was developed on the 150 kilometre-long Middlemarch-Clyde section of line after the railway closed in 1990.

Opposite: End of the line: The railway from Nelson ran a short distance past Glenhope but only briefly. Glenhope then became the terminus of this "rail to nowhere". The line closed in 1955 but the Glenhope Station remains a symbol of Nelson's dream to join the country's rail network.

some dollars by providing beds, meals and side-trips for the trail blazers were appealing.

I stop at ice-cold Oturehua in 2008 and ask hotel proprietor Carol Millar what effect the rail trail is having there. She beams as she cites sales of 180 cut lunches on a typical spring or summer day. She refers also to three backpacker lodges opening in the village, several homestays on nearby farms and minibus excursions to heritage gold towns St Bathans and Naseby.

That's not bad for a township that farmer Barry Becker says was built in the wrong place. Becker, whose forebears settled here over 100 years ago, explains that the original site surveyed for Oturehua was four kilometres to the north. But one frosty morning a train coming down the line was unable to stop on the icy rails and overran the station. The train eventually rolled to a rest and there the pragmatic pioneers decided the town should be shifted.

The rail trail does not go through Ophir but this quaint old gold town benefits hugely from it. Visiting Ophir in 2011 I meet Lois and Bill Galer. They retired from work in Dunedin and moved into their crib (bach) at Ophir permanently. They found life there very quiet at first. The rail trail changed that. With hundreds of cyclists a day riding through Omakau, just five minutes away across the Manuherikia River, they saw their opportunity.

The Galers bought a former shearers' quarters and developed it as a backpackers' lodge. They put publicity leaflets proclaiming the heritage buildings of Ophir, the rumpled gold workings and the smell of wild thyme, into Omakau's former railway station. A year later business was so brisk they felt forced to retire again. There was no shortage of prospective buyers for their old shearers' quarters.

The response is similar at Middlemarch. I call there in 2006 and stay the night at Blind Billy's Holiday Camp (with a name like that, you sort of have to). Middlemarch is the changeover point between the rail trail and the Taieri Gorge excursion train ride. Camp owner Bill Theyers reckons about half the

"trail hounds" stay a night or more at his camp. He counted 3000 guests in 2005.

With figures like that, and numbers increasing yearly, the rail trail idea has proved itself a good one. So good that, when a trail was mooted for the former Christchurch to Little River railway "corridor", who should be happy to address meetings of local farmers and extol the virtues of rail trails but a group of Central Otago farmers?

Perhaps their view on the benefits of rail trails helped promote the "other" Central Otago trail too. Nearing completion in 2015, this trail uses the former Clarksville (near Milton) to Roxburgh branch line. A non-rail section extends it to Alexandra. People I speak to at Waitahuna, Lawrence, Beaumont and Roxburgh sound enthusiastic about it. The Millers Flat community hopes trail hounds will pop into their store and hotel after visiting the Lonely Graves site nearby.

That melancholy patch of dirt above the Clutha River is where lone gold digger William Rigney buried the unidentified body of a man that seemed to have been washed up on a beach of the river. Rigney erected a wooden headstone above the grave. It named the departed simply as "somebody's darling". Rigney later left instructions that, after his own death, he should be buried next to the mystery man.

Millers Flat local historian Betty Adams sees a consistent trickle of visitors driving up the shingle road from the township, past her house, to savour the poignancy of the Lonely Graves. It seems likely "somebody's darling" must have fallen off one of the several gold dredges that worked the Clutha, Adams says.

She talks also about the final days of the Roxburgh branch line. The line reached Millers Flat in 1925. By the time she could remember, only goods trains were running. However, a special passenger train was put on to mark the closing of the line in 1969. She joined a crowd of local people on an excursion to Lawrence for a picnic.

Keeping the rails on the Taieri Gorge section of the Otago Central line for the regular excursion train has been a great success.

Unfortunately the same cannot be said of the excursion service on part of the former Lumsden-Kingston line. The tourist train drawn by the vintage steam locomotive Kingston Flyer from Kingston to Fairlight and back has been plagued by poor patronage. Its operation has been suspended several times. At the time of writing, it seems unlikely to resume.

A Kingston rail enthusiast (not enthusiastic about his name being published though) tells me the old loco has been put up for sale a few times. Locals fear it will be bought and taken elsewhere, such as to the Invercargill-Bluff line. But it belongs at Kingston, he says. It needs Kingston and Kingston needs it.

Once the line from Invercargill to Kingston, via Lumsden, was an integral part of one of New Zealand's biggest tourist attractions. Kingston sits at the southern end of Lake Wakatipu. Passengers leaving their train there boarded a steamboat that chugged up the lake to the popular resort of Queenstown. This trip was so highly regarded it became almost a fashion parade where the "best and richest" had to be seen.

The Kingston rail enthusiast tells me the original Flyer was introduced on the line in 1900. The passenger express could "really fly". Its maximum speed was a death-defying 60kmh.

The renowned steamboat Earnslaw was built in Dunedin. It was transported in pieces by rail to Kingston and entered service on the lake in 1912. It still steams across the lake regularly, carrying tourists from around the world.

Opposite: In a case of recycling for cycling, the Little River railway branch line has been converted to a riding, jogging and walking track. The track skirts part of the shore of Lake Ellesmere and the southern hills of Banks Peninsula, then runs beside Lake Forsyth before entering the township of Little River.

Below: The "Lady of the Lake" graces the catwalk in fashionable Queenstown, against a backdrop of the Remarkable Mountains. TSS Earnslaw has been carrying tourists on Lake Wakatipu for more than a century. Built in Dunedin in 1912, the twin-screw vessel is the only steam-powered ship still in paying passenger service anywhere in the world.

CHAPTER 4

Big ideas

YOU MIGHT WONDER what a Scottish miner, an Australian aviator, a British Governor-General, a North Canterbury farmer, four Southland car salesmen and a group of Nelson pacifists had in common.

One bunch of such disparate characters shared an affinity for "Big Ideas".

People who have big ideas are often mocked as their notions fizzle out to nothing. But for some, their ideas lead to greatness. Whether these people be seen as fizzlers or famous, they contributed to the tapestry of South Island heritage.

Let us consider the Scottish miner first. His name was Peter McSkimming. I discovered his story the day I read a sign pointing to Benhar and turned off the highway to explore this little town for Heartland in 2008.

The road, just north of Balclutha, runs through rolling downs country to a peaceful valley bisected by the main trunk railway. In this cleft of the hills lies the unusual village of Benhar. Seeing it for the first time reminded me at once of that 1960s song about "little boxes on the hillside, little boxes all the same".

The houses are all of red brick and similar in age, size and style. At the base of the valley stand the remains of a large industrial complex. The whole scene is dominated by a very tall brick chimney.

I ask a woman unpacking groceries from her car if anyone could tell me about Benhar and she directs me to John and Julie Posthumus. So I knock on their door. When it opens, a wonderful story opens too. John explains the McSkimming pottery plant was based here. It produced toilet bowls, wash basins, earthenware kitchen vessels and china ornaments for about a century. Part of the works burned down in 1990. The company was then taken over by an Auckland firm and the business joined the drift of many Otago manufacturing interests to the winterless north.

John's Dutch immigrant father worked at the pottery in the 1950s and 1960s and raised his family in one of the company's houses that had so impressed me on first view. Sweet memories of his early life in the company village drew John back to live here with his wife, Julie. Using his father's old scrapbooks of newspaper clippings about Benhar, he launched into documenting the village's history.

Peter McSkimming came to New Zealand in the 1860s and tried his hand as a gold miner.

Opposite: The large, flightless, extinct moa can still be seen at Waikari, North Canterbury. This specimen is not real, of course, but a major find of moa bones in nearby Pyramid Valley was very real. It appeared the giant birds had become trapped in a puggy swamp, possibly trying to evade the clutches of the New Zealand eagle whose bones were also found there.

Above: Smokeless chimney: The large kiln at McSkimming's pottery in Benhar, near Balclutha, was never used for its original purpose. Company founder Peter McSkimming, a devout Presbyterian, would not let the fire burn on the Sabbath and burning only six days a week was impracticable.

Opposite: Cold kiln: The large kiln at McSkimming's pottery was never fired up as long as the McSkimming factory operated. It was used only for storage until the company moved to the North Island. Later, a potter suggested establishing a centre here for amateur potters to work in a cooperative function but the idea died. A start on demolition was made but heritage enthusiasts stopped it.

He then worked in coal mines before going into brick and tile production. He eventually ran several brick works in Otago and the big pottery works at Benhar.

McSkimming was something of a benevolent dictator and a feudal lord. A Presbyterian of powerful virtue, he built the village for his work force and ruled over it majestically. Smoking and drinking were banned. Attendance at divine service in the church, which he built, was compulsory.

A stern figure, but he cared for his people. He housed them well, singles as well as married couples. He provided leisure outlets for them and gave them gifts on their birthdays.

McSkimming's "big idea" came a cropper when he erected a large kiln building with that tall chimney attached. All were made of his own bricks.

John and Julie smile as they get to the nub of the story. They say the new kiln was imported and assembled in 1894. Only when it was ready for use did McSkimming discover that the fire in it must never be allowed to go out. It must burn continuously, even on the Sabbath (Sundays).

The god-fearing McSkimming would have none of that sinfulness – he made sure the new kiln was never fired up. The building that housed it was used only for storage. No smoke ever sullied the chimney. The pottery continued to rely on its old kiln.

A Balclutha businesswoman bought the kiln in 1992 and began to dismantle the chimney so she could put the bricks up for sale. John, Julie and many other locals were outraged at the potential loss of a heritage structure. They organised a demonstration that attracted many participants. The angry crowd joined hands to form a ring of protest around the building. Authorities then stepped in and the historic site was saved.

The businesswoman was fined heavily for non-consented demolition and had to restore

the little damage she had already done. So, the chimney still stands like a sentinel over McSkimming's former fiefdom.

Crash-landing his plane in a South Westland swamp was not what Australian aviator Guy Menzies' set out to do. But in doing it, he achieved his "big idea", to make the first solo crossing of the Tasman Sea by air.

His venture ended in La Fontaine swamp, near the town of Hari Hari, in 1931. The marshy ground stopped his plane so abruptly that it tipped "tail over kite", leaving Menzies suspended upside-down by his safety harness. It was an ignominious end to an epic and successful flight.

Menzies had set out from Sydney's Mascot Aerodrome in his single-engined plane and, recording an average speed of 160kmh, "touched down" fully 12 hours later. The flight might have been slightly shorter had bad weather in the Southern Alps not forced him to turn back from his plan to land in Canterbury. He became lost in heavy cloud and flew around seeking somewhere on the West Coast to put

his plane down. Spotting a patch of level green ground below, he decided to land.

Lesson one – never trust level green ground as a suitable landing strip in South Westland.

Menzies was unhurt and the local community was overjoyed. He became the centre of celebrations up and down the Coast. How dismayed the Coasters must have felt a decade later when their hero, by then an air force squadron leader in World War II, was shot down over Italy and killed.

Somehow, Menzies never quite attracted the public adulation that fellow Australian Charles Kingsford-Smith had in his aircraft, Southern Cross, three years earlier. "Smithie", as he was known, made the first trans-Tasman flight, landing in Christchurch. But he had a crew of three and a plane powered by three engines.

Menzies called his plane Southern Cross Junior, in recognition of Kingsford-Smith's feat. A replica of the little biplane stands in a display shelter beside the highway through Hari Hari.

After looking at the replica in 2011, I drove 10 kilometres across the lush Hari Hari plain to the swamp where Menzies landed. The ground there has been drained and cows now graze on it. A monument to Menzies was erected at the edge of the cow paddock on the 75th anniversary of Menzies' landing, in 2006.

Hari Hari has been through bad times since the 1980s, when its giant sawmill closed. Community leaders are trying to find tourist attractions that might boost numbers of visitors stopping in the town. They see Menzies' landing site as something that might appeal to visitors.

Hotelier John McCaul tells me the town has plans to market itself on an aviation theme. This should include using the farm paddock where Menzies landed as a destination for members of the Aeroplane Owners' and Pilots' Association, McCaul says. He sees the location as an ideal base for flying enthusiasts to traverse the skies over magnificent mountains, lakes, bush and sea. Many flyers would come. Hari Hari's motels, pubs, eateries and stores would benefit greatly, McCaul says.

Well, maybe. I just hope the flying strangers don't deviate from the landing approach, miss the drained paddock, and tip "tail over kite" into swampland.

Right: Landing strip: Guy Menzies made a soft landing in this Hari Hari, South Westland, paddock. Too soft. His plane bogged so abruptly that it flipped over. But The Australian aviator was not hurt or dismayed. He had just completed the first solo flight from Australia to New Zealand, in 1931.

Below: Ooops! Guy Menzies' plane has flipped over. But nobody cares about that. For, in this sodden South Westland paddock, near Hari Hari, history has been made. And besides, Menzies is not hurt. The Australian aviator and all the West Coast are celebrating the first solo flight between Australia and New Zealand.
Alexander Turnbull Library

GOVERNORS-GENERAL TEND TO have big ideas. Just think of the names Bledisloe and Ranfurly in relation to two of New Zealand's most coveted rugby trophies.

Englishman Lord Cobham also had strong sporting interests. He believed in the power of outdoor activities to develop strong, confident, caring and resourceful young adults. He was keen to establish the international Outward Bound movement in New Zealand when he was appointed Governor-General in 1957.

It didn't take him long. In 1962, Cobham formed a trust that prepared the way for New Zealand's Outward Bound school. The site they chose was the bush-fringed cove of Anakiwa, near the head of Marlborough's Queen Charlotte Sound.

Taking the road that curls beside the upper reaches of the sound to peaceful Anakiwa in 2011, I see a group of 14 students rowing their cutter home from a day of marine exercises. And I think, they could be the grandchildren of original course members.

Also watching their movements is Central Otago farmer David Small. He did the Outward Bound course in 1970. He still values the experience and says he has maintained high levels of physical fitness ever since. He and his wife have just hiked the Queen Charlotte Track. He could not leave the area without returning to Anakiwa to see how it is going.

Above: Anakiwa's classroom is the sea and the bush. Outward Bound activities in this part of Queen Charlotte Sound challenge course members to push themselves to their limits and discover their inner strength.

In 1970 he was an active, sports-mad late-teenager.

"I loved every second of it," he says of Outward Bound. He notes changes in the physical environment and is pleased to see women students are now included in the course. But he feels sure the essential values of the place and the course remain unchanged.

Small's brow furrows in a frown as he remembers a few students who came unwillingly in 1970. Sponsored by businesses, aged around 30, they were smokers and overweight. It was tough for them, he says. Looking at the current crop of students as they bump the cutter against the wharf, he sees none of that unfortunate type.

Course directors confer on the wharf as the students make their weary way up to the spacious Outward Bound buildings that nestle below the hills. I can't help envying them a little, and admiring Cobham a lot.

Above: Serenity surrounds the headquarters building of Outward Bound in a tranquil corner of Queen Charlotte Sound. But the peace is shattered daily as people on the course are put through their paces at a strenuous rate. Activities up mountains, in bush and on the sea challenge them to push themselves to their limits.

Below: Inward bound: These students of the Outward Bound School at Anakiwa, in the Marlborough Sounds, are returning from a day's exertions on the water. The school, promoted by former Governor-General Viscount Cobham, aims to develop personal qualities of confidence, initiative, leadership and teamwork.

Joseph Hodgen's "big idea" was really not so big at all. But the ramifications of it were huge.

The farmer at Pyramid Valley, near Hawarden in North Canterbury, simply set out in 1938 to bury a horse that had died. A big horse, yes, one that had drawn Hodgen's farm cart, loaded with hay bales and fence posts, around the hilly property for many years. So, the hole for the horse's carcass had to be big too.

A dried swamp, where the top was still soft, seemed a good place to dig. Hodgen and his son, Rob, set to work there with shovel and crowbar. Pretty soon they unearthed three large and unusual bones.

Rob's wife, Molly, tells me in 2011, that her husband and father-in-law realised the bones were not those of any animal they were familiar with. They reckoned they must be moa bones. They contacted David Hope, a friend and ornithologist. He confirmed their theory and then, probing the swamp with a long, thin spear, found more moa bones.

Hope surmised that the giant birds had probably been foraging for food in this area and had become stuck in the swamp. It would have sucked them down and then preserved the bones in excellent condition.

Molly describes the swamp to me as a thick jelly that wobbled when you jumped on it. So, jellied moa anyone?

Canterbury Museum certainly wanted some. This was a find of international importance. Museum staff began excavations in 1939. By the time they stopped, in 1979, they had recovered the equivalent of about 200 complete bird skeletons. Most of the bones were of moa.

Included among the bones were some of the extinct New Zealand eagle. This led me to visions of the eagle preying on the poor, clumsy moa until the swamp claimed them for its own.

Humble Heriot hardly seems the place to inspire big ideas. Yet a family reputed at one time to be New Zealand's richest came from Heriot, a township that basks in picturesque rolling farm country 25km north-east of Gore, in West Otago.

They were the Todd family, people of initiative, drive and such social conscience that they never forgot or forsook their humble beginnings. Their generosity to Heriot, even after they had left the area, was legendary.

Charles Todd toiled on the Central Otago goldfields until 1864, when he moved south to Heriot. The settlement was just seven years old. The surrounding hills and valleys had been cleared and large sheep runs were beginning to prosper. Soon much of the land would be divided up for family farms based on the romney sheep breed.

Sensing the promise of the district, Todd established a wool scour and a fellmongery at Heriot. He later added a stock and station agency and a large grain store to his business empire.

Son Charles eventually took over his father's business interests. Charles and his wife had four sons. These lads, raised in a simple whitewashed cottage, were to become known throughout New Zealand as Todd Brothers.

Many people still remember this as a national trade name linked to motoring. Why?

The brothers were avid car fanciers in the early days of motoring. They owned the first car in the Heriot area, from 1908. They popularised motor transport and opened a garage in the small town for the repair, maintenance and hire of motor vehicles. Next they gained the franchise to import Ford models from the United States. These cars came in parts, packed in crates. The Todds assembled them and sold them, from Heriot to all parts of the country.

Over the years Heriot's remoteness began to present problems in a growing and increasingly competitive market. The Todds moved to the cities in the 1920s. They moved also into exploration for oil and natural gas. They expanded their car assembly business, becoming New Zealand's major distributor of the Rootes Group line of cars and trucks from England: Humbers, Hillmans, Commers and Karriers. When Japanese vehicles started to make their mark in New Zealand, Todds switched to the Mitsubishi brand.

Meanwhile, back in Heriot, the Todd family's vintage cottage still looks as good as new when I visit in 2007. That is partly because it is still owned by Todd family descendants.

George and Nola Garrett tell me how they bought the cottage in 1964 but sold it back to the Todds in 1978. Bryan Todd restored it, then leased it back to them. They are very much at home in it and are proud to show me through the "living museum" which they keep meticulously clean and tidy.

Under the Garretts' care, and the protection of the Historic Places Trust, the simple whitewashed home has become an attraction to pilgrims of the motoring sort.

There is not much else in Heriot these days. Once it was the end of a railway branch line that ran from Waipahi on the main trunk, through Tapanui. There was talk of it being extended to Roxburgh. All of that has gone now. In place of the railway yards is the sprawling depot of a large trucking firm – a common symbol of the decline of rural towns in the modern age.

Local farmer Peter Herbert's study of the area's history has filled him with admiration for the Todd family. He says farming has always

been the backbone of Heriot. But sometimes that backbone has needed a little financial massaging from the stock and station firms.

Companies such as Todd Brothers carried their clients through hard times, Herbert says.

"They were very genuine people. They had a sound relationship with their staff and were very generous," he adds.

Down the main street sad verandas tilt against empty shops. But my abiding vision of Heriot in 2007 is the large grain store building beside the former railway. On a wall, in faded letters, I can just decipher the sign, "Todd Brothers". I hope it will still be legible next time I call.

ERNLE CLARK HAD A "big idea", though he thought little of it at the time. Had he been more ambitious, or vain, he might well have beaten Jean Batten to be the first person to fly from England to New Zealand.

Instead, he was the second. Not that it worried him. He simply said, "Well, no one remembers who comes second, do they?" And, sadly, he was right. For, when I discover his story in 2012 and run it as a Heartland column in *The Press*, many puzzled calls came from readers wanting to know more about this man lost in the mists of history.

Clark's story does bear telling. For, if the flying farmer from Scargill Valley in North Canterbury had beaten Batten, it would have come as a surprise to him. He was unconcerned about her attempt to be the first, possibly even unaware of it. He had no intention of racing her, or anyone else, to make the marathon flight.

I find information about Clark on interpretation boards erected along the Ernle Clark Walkway, which meanders through native bush beside the Heathcote River in Christchurch. The bush reserve stands on the former Thorrington farm where Clark grew up. The wider area, now densely residential, is still known as Thorrington.

Above: George Garrett is proud to live in a cottage with a Historic Place designation. This simple house at Heriot, West Otago, was the home of the Todd family. Todd Brothers became a major national corporation – and it all began here.

Opposite: For Kiwi business magnates the Todd Brothers, it all began with a motor garage in the small West Otago town of Heriot. This photo from a century ago shows the Todds' hankering for motor vehicles of two and four-wheeled varieties. They brought motoring, first to Otago, then to New Zealand. But they never forgot Heriot.
Todd Family Collection

Clark took up farming near Scargill, an hour north of Christchurch. He learned to fly with the Canterbury Aero Club and qualified as a pilot in 1934. Two years later he accompanied his mother and his brother on the long sea trip to England to visit relatives.

While in England he looked around for a suitable plane to buy. He spotted a single-engined Percival monoplane for sale and decided he would have it.

His plan then was to disassemble and pack the plane into a crate and ship it home to Lyttelton. But the more he thought of it, the more inclined he felt to fly it home. And why not? Sure, such a flight had never been done before but if he split the journey into short stages, he could see no reason why he couldn't manage it.

So, a change of plan was Clark's "big idea". And packing some food and drink, an atlas and a compass, he took off. His planned route of eight stages took him over stormy oceans, rugged mountains, windswept deserts, steaming jungles and places where the inhabitants might not be too friendly. At each stop he refuelled and rested before taking to the air again.

Over the Australian outback he flew low enough to navigate by following a railway line. Then he struck smoke from bushfires that blacked out his view. It must have been a nervous time but he was not one to panic. At last he found his way again and landed at Sydney.

By this time Clark's flight had been in the news and he was surprised to be greeted as a celebrity. He took a few days off in Sydney to visit friends, before leaving on the final stage, to Christchurch.

Word of his pending arrival preceded him and a crowd of thousands turned out at Wigram aerodrome to welcome him home. His trip had taken 20 days.

It is said that only when he climbed down from his plane did he learn that Jean Batten's 11-day flight had ended at her home town of Rotorua a month earlier. She had left England three weeks before him.

The reception Clark got in Canterbury reflected that given to Guy Menzies who had made the first trans-Tasman solo flight only five years earlier. Clark, by nature a quiet, unassuming Kiwi, returned to his farm. But a further similarity to Menzies was to follow.

In World War II, Clark enlisted with the air force. He won promotion from flying officer to squadron leader. He was decorated with the Distinguished Flying Cross for carrying out hazardous photo-reconnaissance missions over enemy territory.

That territory was probably more hazardous than his long route home from England in 1936. However, unlike Menzies, Clark survived the war. He later married and raised a family on a farm near Darfield.

There is a happy (for me) postscript to his story. After my account of it ran in *The Press*, one of Clark's sons rang me. He just wanted to say how much his family appreciated that their father was, at last, receiving public recognition.

A STATUE OF JOHN GRIGG stands in Ashburton. People pass it with barely a glance. Yet Grigg could rightly be considered the "father" of the Mid Canterbury district. His ideas were really big.

Grigg was a Cornish emigrant with farming experience who landed at Auckland at the time of the New Zealand land wars. He went into market gardening to supply food for the fast-growing town and prospered. Then he bought a large block of land far away from the inter-race troubles. In Mid Canterbury, in 1864, he established his farm, Longbeach.

The land was bordered roughly on the south by the Hinds River and on the north by the Ashburton River, on the east by the ocean and the west by the road that ran between Christchurch and Timaru. Yes, it was big, but it was also wet. Too wet to grow crops. People who knew about land said it was useless.

Grigg knew it need not be useless if it was drained. He found good deposits of clay, set up a brick kiln near them and turned out miles of tile pipes. He cut ditches, laid pipes and drained the land of its lying water. Thus he developed a farm that people who knew about agriculture came to call "the most famous farm in the world".

Right: Who is this stern Victorian gent gazing over all who pass beneath him in central Ashburton? That is John Grigg, in statue form of course. From 1864 he developed the famous Longbeach station and a farmstead that was a veritable village. He was a benevolent boss to his staff of 200 and they respected him highly.

Opposite: Ernle Clark was the proud owner of a Percival Gull aeroplane. Soon he would record an amazing flight in it. The humble Scargill, North Canterbury, farmer flew the Gull solo from England to New Zealand in 1936. His 20-day exploit ended at Wigram Airfield, a month after Jean Batten had become the first to fly solo from England to New Zealand.

Bit by bit Grigg's holdings grew to a total size of 32,000 acres. More than a farm, it was a mini-republic in which 200 men lived and worked and raised families. Many of the families resided in two townships on Grigg land – around the Longbeach homestead block and at Waterton a few miles away. Grigg established the latter because he recognised the need for workers to have their private lives separate from their workplaces.

For Grigg, though he might have seemed the president of his republic, was a humanitarian. His treatment of staff was summed up in a saying he used often: "No one works for John Grigg – they work on Longbeach." That is why few workers ever left to try their luck elsewhere. Some families stayed at Longbeach for several generations.

His descendants have maintained this tradition, through good times and bad. They added a stylish new homestead that hosted the newly crowned Queen Elizabeth and her husband Prince Philip for a weekend on their first Royal Tour of New Zealand in the summer of 1953-1954.

My visit to Longbeach in 2011 is more low-key. The district council does not seal the road for me, as it did for the royal couple. Still, I get a warm feeling from being in the homestead, designed by Christchurch architect Heathcote Helmore, where the Queen and Duke relaxed from their duties. I can almost hear the Queen's murmured prayer as I enter the homestead chapel where she attended Sunday service.

Owners Bill and Penny Thomas are committed to the conservation of the farmstead buildings. They plan to open them to visitors and for functions. They are as proud of the restored original sod cottage as of the well maintained chapel, stables, cookhouse, blacksmith shop, dairy, killing shed, and the expansive gardens.

Bill is a direct descendant, through his mother, of the original John Grigg. But he knows there must be changes. The farm is not as big as it once was. Raising sheep and crops is more intensive but it makes sense to diversify further. Part of the farm has been converted to dairying. So, instead of draining water, Bill is spraying it onto paddocks from giant irrigators.

IF EVER A MAN DREAMED BIG, that man was Robert Campbell. His legacy includes a Scottish baronial-style house at the foot of lofty North Otago hills in the Waitaki Valley. This imposing structure is known to locals as "the castle".

Campbell was "king of the castle" and one of New Zealand's wealthiest runholders in the late 19th century. Among his acquisitions was Otekaieke Station. It had been owned previously by William Dansey who lived in a cave and after whom the Dansey Pass was named. The pass links Duntroon in North Otago with Naseby in Central Otago.

A later owner of Otekaieke built a homestead in the 1860s. When I visit in 2012, Mike and Wendy Bayley are living in it. The couple own and manage Otekaieke Station, though it is much reduced after government purchase of land and subdivision into smaller farms around 1900.

Wendy's connection with Otekaieke goes back three generations to 1913, when her grandfather bought the station. Otekaieke stayed in the Munro family's hands for many years and Wendy grew up there. She tells me that when Campbell bought the station, he considered living in this homestead was beneath his dignity. He had plans drawn up by top architects for "the castle" and travelled to Europe to hire craftsmen builders and buy items for the project. The craftsmen returned with him and brought his dream of a baronial manor to reality in 1876.

A village of farm buildings and workers' cottages grew up around it and Campbell lived the life of a lord. But kingdoms tumble in time and, after the death of Campbell and his wife, childless, in their 40s, the government bought "the castle". It was used as a kind of borstal, then a residential corrective school for boys from all parts of New Zealand. More houses were added to the complex for the teaching staff of 70.

Liz Matson lived in one of these houses with her teacher husband, John, and their children in the 1960s. The complex was by then known as Campbell Park. Matson tells me she became interested in the Campbell history and found that Campbell and his wife used to host many social events. It seems his early death was brought on at least partly by over-indulgence in alcohol.

So, from a cave to a castle, Otekaieke was a big idea indeed. When I see it in 2012, entry is forbidden by its American owners. They have tried to establish an international school here but without success. Most of the houses around it are rented by farm workers up the Waitaki Valley.

At time of writing, Otekaieke is back on the market awaiting a multi-millionaire to come up with some other idea for its use.

Opposite: The Queen and Duke of Edinburgh stayed at Longbeach, on the Mid-Canterbury coast. Bill and Penny Thomas are staying there too. As descendants of pioneer John Grigg, who founded and developed "the world's best farm", the Thomases now own and manage the farm. Determined to protect its heritage, they have restored such buildings as the old cookhouse (pictured).

"Big ideas" are not confined to individual people. A list of South Island ventures that began with multiples of people "putting their heads together" could go on almost forever. Let's look at a few notable ones that I have come across in my Heartland travels.

Pacifism is a "big idea", even more so in a time of war. At Riverside, near Motueka, during World War II, a group of women pacifists felt a pressing need to support one another and their children.

Their menfolk had been arrested for refusing conscription to the military services. As conscientious objectors, they had been locked up in crude camps far away in the North Island. There they cut scrub and were treated as convicts.

The women protested loudly against compulsory military service for the men. Their protests drew insults and threats from other people, some of whom had husbands, brothers, boyfriends and sons serving in the armed forces.

Many of the pacifist women were church-going Methodists. They sought security in their Motueka congregation from the baying crowd. A fellow Methodist, Hubert Holdaway, saw their need and let them settle on a patch of land he owned by the Moutere River at Lower Moutere.

Soon a community of families and like-minded others were living there and attending services at the local Methodist church. Thus was the Riverside Community born.

Visiting Riverside in 2011, I find it difficult to imagine what must have originally been little more than a spartan camp site. In 70 years the community has built an impressive array of cottages and communal buildings, streets and pathways. It has developed gardens, orchards, a power plant and a small farm, so it is almost self-sufficient. More importantly, at least to me on this hot day, it runs a cafe open to the public where I enjoy a tasty lunch and good coffee.

I ask resident Tristan Vincent how the community became a commune and how it got to this stage. After all, other communes all over New Zealand have risen and fallen in much shorter time – many of them dissolving in scandals of "free love", sexual abuse and exploitation.

Vincent's early life was spent at Riverside. He left to study science at Victoria University, Wellington. After graduating PhD he headed overseas for lecturing and consultancy work.

Right: Communal living suits Tristan Vincent. He was born and raised at Riverside, achieved a doctorate in science at Victoria University, lectured and did consultancy work in Germany, then returned to his roots. Riverside, near Motueka, began as a Methodist community in the 1940s. It is now a non-denominational commune.

Then, with a wife and two children whom he longed to introduce to the lifestyle he had enjoyed as a youngster at Riverside, he came back a decade ago.

This commune was always different from others, Vincent says. It was founded on religious beliefs, including pacifism, and its economy was based on agriculture. Members cleared the land and developed a dairy farm. They also raised sheep and grew cash crops. Residents worked on the farm and it provided an income stream. Many of the members held regular jobs in the wider area. Their wages and the returns from farming were shared equally among the community. Members could have bank accounts but owned very little in the way of private property.

As Vincent tells me this I think of the fleet of slightly battered and ageing Mazda, Nissan and Mitsubishi small cars scattered about the place. They are common property. Members take any available car when one is needed.

Riverside has never had a demi-god ruler. Democracy reigns, with regular meetings of the adult members to consider management issues and resolve them by consensus, Vincent says.

The commune plays active parts in the Lower Moutere and Motueka areas. The children attend schools there and everyone becomes involved in school, cultural and sporting activities. The former Riverside chapel was open to all for worship. Surplus garden and orchard produce is given to the needy.

Is Vincent's view a little rosy? Not really. He speaks just as positively of the gradual move away from the religious base (the chapel has become a gymnasium) to a secular community. He affirms the community, now declining in numbers as members age and fewer new entrants arrive, still holds to its original ethic of shared work and shared returns in a truly Christian way.

It has always been prepared to take up the protest banners, too, just as its founders did to oppose military action in the 1940s. Members since then have joined public protests against national issues ranging from involvement in the Vietnam War to hosting racially selected rugby teams from South Africa.

That should not be surprising. After all, early member Sonja Davies sharpened her political activist teeth in a highly publicised action to stop the closure of Nelson's railway. The action failed but Davies became a national figure in debates over human rights in later years.

ONEKAKA, NORTH OF TAKAKA in Golden Bay, once had a profitable steel mill. Twenty years later, it didn't. Little indication of its size and significance remains for the casual passerby to recognise its existence.

Visiting Golden Bay in 2008, I am taken on a climb into the hills behind Onekaka. Department of Conservation historian Nigel Mountfort drives his 4WD truck as far as it can go on the steep and slushy track. From there we hike upwards until, soaked by drizzle dripping through the bush, we reach the first relics of an aerial ropeway that once carried iron ore from a quarry high on the hill to a smelting plant at its foot.

There, Mountfort explains, the ropeway served the steel mill that operated at Onekaka, north of Takaka, in the 1920s and 1930s. We carry on our climb, past old ropeway fixtures, abandoned ropeway buckets and bits of rock containing iron ore that must have fallen from the buckets on their journey downhill. At last we reach a clearing where the sight of a dam and powerhouse startle me.

The hydro power station was built here to provide electricity for the steel mill, Mountfort says. Quarry workers lived in huts on a high ridge and dug the iron ore from sites at the summit of the hill. Before the ropeway was established, horses dragged supplies up to them on sledges.

Men were tough in those days. But I wonder if their effort was all worthwhile. Yes, says Mountfort, for the steel mill was a success – the first successful steel mill in New Zealand. For nearly two decades newly smelted steel was loaded onto ships from a wharf at Onekaka. Some of the wharf piles are still visible. Nearby is a patch of flat ground where bits of the old mill can also be seen.

Economically, the enterprise was not so successful, though. It always struggled to turn a profit. A major reason was the high cost of transporting top-quality coal from Westport by sea for the smelting process. Added to that was the realisation that ore deposits on the hill were smaller than had been estimated.

The mill was closed just before World War II. There were moves to reopen it when Japan entered the war, in case New Zealand was blockaded and unable to import steel. This came to nothing and Onekaka's "big idea" slipped into oblivion.

Well, not quite oblivion. The little power station continued working for a further decade, before the Golden Bay Electric Power Board dismantled it. But now a new power house has risen at the dam, where a private concern has plans to generate electricity for sale to the national grid.

Left: Where blast furnaces produced iron in the 1920s, native bush has taken over. The Onekaka iron works, north of Takaka in Golden Bay, prospered briefly but declined sharply from the end of that decade. They staggered to a close in the 1950s.

Opposite: Relicts of historic Matanaka stand on a hill overlooking the Pacific Ocean, near Waikouaiti. Whaling captain Johnny Jones brought workers from Australia to establish a farm at Matanaka in 1840 to feed his crews. The farm grew and, by 1848, was able to feed shiploads of settlers arriving at Dunedin.

OTHER BIG IDEAS? The South Island is not short of them. But it could hardly be compared to Texas, even though, like the American state, it once held high hopes of riches from oil wells. On my visits to Kotuku, near Lake Brunner, inland from Greymouth, and to Chertsey, north of Ashburton, I am shown patches of ground where crude oil once seeped to the surface.

Efforts were made at both places to capitalise on the "black gold". Bores were drilled. Tests were carried out. But always the economy of further exploration remained tantalisingly out of reach.

Uranium deposits were found at Gillespies Beach, near Fox Glacier in South Westland. When the Americans began their project to develop atomic bombs in World War II they asked the New Zealand Government to assess the viability of uranium mining at Gillespies Beach. The tests, which were kept secret, discounted the likelihood that the radioactive metal could be recovered in sufficient quantities. Perhaps many New Zealanders were relieved.

Whaling today is about as popular as atomic weaponry. Once, though, it was a flourishing industry. Riverton, in Southland, and Waikouaiti, in Otago, are substantial coastal towns built on whaling.

An interesting place to visit is Matanaka, just outside Waikouaiti. There whaling captain Johnny Jones developed an early farm to feed his large whaling station. Produce from the farm also helped sustain the Scottish pioneers who founded Dunedin in 1848. Some of the farm buildings are open for inspection.

Today's equivalent of these industries is dairying. Fonterra milk processing plants at Clandeboye, north of Timaru, and Edendale, north of Invercargill, are vying for the title of world's largest dairy factory when I visit them for Heartland.

World's biggest – that is about as big as an idea can get.

CHAPTER 5

Cast of characters

CHARLES UPHAM DID NOT want to talk to me. The World War II hero's dislike of publicity was well known. He did not want any.

Sure, he was the only combat soldier to win the Victoria Cross and Bar (the VC medal twice) for gallantry, but he did not accept that this should make him a target for journalists to interview.

However, when Upham sold his farm at Conway Flats, south of Kaikoura, and arranged to move with his wife, Molly, to a retirement home in Christchurch, he agreed to one interview for *The Press*. The editor, bless his golden heart, asked me to do the job.

It was more than a job for me. It was an honour and a privilege, but also a challenge. Realising he might be an unwilling partner, I prepared a little manoeuvre to catch him out. Nothing more than a good army captain, such as he had been, would do on the eve of battle.

Molly greeted me and photographer Dean Kozanic at the door of the farmhouse and ushered us to seats on the front veranda. Then she brought her husband out. He sat down on the two-seater couch beside me and looked staunchly the other way.

Opposite: Each time I cross the Arawhata River south of Haast I look upstream to the mountains and in my mind catch a glimpse of William O'Leary trudging out of the mist with his horse. The story of O'Leary, "Arawata Bill", can have that effect on a person.
Alexander Turnbull Library

After some polite small-talk with Molly, I leaned towards Charles and played my trump card.

"Do you remember Bob May?" I asked.

As a boy growing up in Hawarden I had known Bob May and his sons. I knew he was Upham's close mate. As Upham's sergeant-major, he had carried the severely wounded but wildly protesting Upham to a first-aid post in the thick of battle in the North African desert. He had then taken over Upham's command.

"Yes, I know Bob May," I said, and I explained how I knew him. At that moment, Upham grasped my wrist in his vice-like farmer's hand and said to his wife, "Molly, this man knows Bob May". The interview proceeded from that point. The only difficulty was that Upham did not let go of my wrist, which prevented me from taking notes. So the story was not a great piece of writing but I can claim it was a remarkable feat of memory.

Upham died not long after moving to Bishopspark retirement home in Christchurch. My interview might have been the last one he ever gave. He did not reveal much. We just chatted about the farm and his life in peace time. Upham was not inclined to talk about the war and I had to respect that.

Some months later I spotted May while I was visiting the Rannerdale War Veterans' Home in Christchurch to interview someone else.

Above: Charles Upham was New Zealand's most highly decorated soldier, with two Victoria Cross awards for actions in World War II. Upham shunned attention and had a distaste for personal publicity. He did agree, however, to one interview for *The Press* on his last day at his Conway Flats farm before entering a Christchurch retirement home. He died a few weeks later.

Dean Kozanic Fairfax Media NZ/The Press

We had a quick chat in which I described how I had used his name to get Upham talking. May seemed amused that his old mate had fallen for my ploy. He did not mind me using his name. He just chuckled and said: "Bloody old Charlie".

I asked May if he would talk to me about the war. He stared at me and his face clouded. Then he replied: "Mike, I was too young then, and I'm too old now". That was it – subject closed.

Some time after Upham's death, his family held a dedication service at his grave in the churchyard of St Paul's, Papanui, in Christchurch. I went along to cover the event for *The Press*. One of his daughters told me Bob May had been invited to place a wreath on the grave but he had not turned up. She was clearly concerned so, back at the office, I phoned Rannerdale to see if he was ill. No, said the receptionist. She had seen him getting into the taxi to go to the service that morning.

I puzzled over this until I met a friend of Upham's and asked him if he knew what had

happened that morning. He broke into laughter and told me that May had got into the taxi and was riding down Riccarton Road when he suddenly told the taxi driver to stop. He ordered the driver to turn around and take him back to the Bush Inn, a pub near Rannerdale.

May had later explained to Upham's family that he felt Charlie would have been happier having a beer than having flowers on his grave.

UPHAM AND MAY are just two of the dozens of war veterans I interviewed, though not for the Heartland column. People often ask me about the characters I met in my job. Then my thoughts turn to Upham and May. But there are many other interesting characters.

Some of them are well known. Some are obscure. Some I met in person and interviewed. Others were long dead before I came along and their stories were told to me by people who knew of their deeds and their idiosyncrasies. Let us consider a few who featured in Heartland over the 10 years that the column ran.

RUNNING EARLY TO AN INTERVIEW one day in 2010, I stop at Little River, on Banks Peninsula. I enter the shop and buy a ginger beer. As I walk out, I see a car parked near the door and know instantly the woman in the front passenger seat is Nancy Duxbury.

We have never met. I have never seen her photograph. But it must be her. And it is.

Her age gives her away. She is about to turn 100. This former school teacher is being taken by an ex-pupil, Des McSweeney, back to the vacant site of the Holmes Bay School, as a birthday treat. It has been arranged for me to interview her on the grassy paddock where the school was open for just eight years, in the 1930s and 1940s.

Miss Duxbury (even in his 80s, retired Lincoln University lecturer McSweeney still calls his old teacher by her formal name) taught at Holmes Bay for seven of those eight years. She was "at home" there. She had been born and raised round the corner at Pigeon Bay.

As part of the 100th birthday treat, McSweeney has got farmer Pam Richardson to put on a picnic for Duxbury on the old school site. Richardson spreads a chequered table cloth on the ground and lays out the farm-baked goodies, while McSweeney arranges the centenarian in a deck chair. Then the reminiscing begins.

Duxbury remembers there were only 12 children at the school, from four families. She boarded with each family in turn, so got to know her pupils well. The four fathers had assembled the kitset school building that the Canterbury Education Board had sent over by boat.

Oh they were great days: family picnics at the wharf on Sundays, school inspectors trudging the gravel road on foot to visit the school, the school gardens lovingly tended by the children, little contact with other peninsula communities, a weekly steamship bringing supplies from Lyttelton and taking farm produce back, hard-up families in the Depression picking cocksfoot along the roadside for cash, possum carcases hanging on the school gate.

The children used to kill the possums and hang them on the gate where a local trapper collected them. This provided the kids' pocket money, Duxbury explains.

The school roll dropped, the education board closed the school, the kitset building was taken away. Now the Richardsons' sheep graze where the children used to play.

Duxbury shifted to Christchurch. Judging by responses to the Heartland column on Holmes Bay, she must have made as big an impression in the big, tough city schools as she had in tranquil Holmes Bay. Several ex-pupils contacted me to extol her inspirational teaching.

ONCE A KEEN RUNNER, I was a big fan of Dave McKenzie. The little red-head from Dunollie, near Greymouth, was probably New Zealand's greatest marathon runner.

It amazes me to find how few people today know of him. Perhaps I should not be amazed. For McKenzie is the personification of modesty. In the true amateur days of the 1960s, with no sponsors or promoters, he stunned the athletics world. But his shyness and humility would not allow him to bathe in glory.

Knowing he is like this, I approach McKenzie in his humble home in the small coalmining town fearing he will not have much to say. But once he finds I am interested in running, he warms up. Soon he is producing scrapbooks and photographs from a cupboard. Next we are poring over them like a pair of old mates.

Dunollie is almost connected to Runanga. The twin coal towns sit at the foot of hills that reach up to the coal-rich Paparoa Range. Coal is in McKenzie's blood, which may explain his stubbornness, determination, independence and resistance to pain.

His job was as a printer at the *Greymouth Star* newspaper. His joy was in sports, mainly running. He devised his own training schedules, beginning with runs in his (extended) lunch hour, followed by running home after work (10 kilometres) and then some serious

Below: New Zealand's greatest, and probably most modest, marathon runner has lived all his life in the coal mining town of Dunollie, near Greymouth. His street number 42 happens to be also the number of kilometres in a marathon.

distances in the evening. All this in whatever weather the West Coast could deliver. And you know what that means!

By the mid-1960s he was churning out world-class times over various distances in road and cross-country races. His marathon times would rank him well among New Zealand's best runners today.

Ever loyal to his Greymouth athletics club, where he has coached and mentored youngsters, McKenzie turned up at the start of the 1967 Boston Marathon in the club's green singlet with a yellow G over the left breast. No one knew anything about him. He laughs heartily when recalling that one American radio sports commentator, puzzled by the G, could only surmise that he was representing Greece.

Boston was the most prestigious of world marathons outside the Olympics. In 1967 it attracted the world's best runners in a field of 700. McKenzie was able to compete only because generous West Coasters had donated to a fund to get him there. The race was run in cold, driving rain and sleet on an undulating course. That might have suited McKenzie, even though he wore several T-shirts under his Greymouth singlet. He won easily and in race record time of 2 hours, 15 minutes, 45 seconds. Then, as soon as possible, he disappeared from the limelight.

This, of course, made the American sports media even more voracious. Suddenly, this "nobody" from "nowhere" was splashed all over the newspapers. Suddenly, too, reporters began digging for information. They found this diminutive Kiwi, from the same little country that had recently produced Olympic champion runners Murray Halberg and Peter Snell, had already won successive New Zealand Marathon titles, in 1966 and 1967.

One story the reporters would have loved to get was that McKenzie's inspiration at Boston was the memory of his brother, Hector, killed

Above: Memories of marathons: Top long-distance runner Dave McKenzie of Dunollie, near Greymouth, was legendary for "letting his deeds do the talking". Now in retirement, he allows himself to pore over old newspaper headlines that acclaim his achievements.

in the Strongman Mine disaster a few months previously.

McKenzie won a long succession of Canterbury titles. He ran his fastest time of 2 hours, 12 minutes, 26 seconds when coming third in the 1967 Japan Marathon. However, further appearances on the international stage were limited by injuries. He was selected to run for New Zealand at the Mexico and Munich Olympics but was unplaced. He was forced to withdraw from the Jamaica Commonwealth Games.

Few New Zealand runners could match his record. So I notice a wince and a wistful light in his eye as he points to a low fence across the street from his Dunollie home. He explains that, heading off on a training run one evening with his dog on a lead, he was startled when another dog charged at them. He became tangled in the lead and tripped while trying to clear that fence. He suffered concussion, a broken arm, a smashed knee and a head gash that required stitches.

It is too tempting to say injuries dogged his career.

THE OLD SONG "HARD TIMES, hard times come again no more" could have been Robin Robilliard's anthem. The bluesy lyrics could have summed up her life. But that would be to ignore her later years when her activities ensured an easy retirement for herself and her hard-working husband, Garry.

I meet Robbie, as she is known, through the pages of her book, *Hard Country*, in 2014. It is such a stirring read that I make a point of meeting her in person. In her I find a sprightly and enthusiastic woman of about 80, going on 30.

Robbie threw away a life of wealth and luxury in the lap of her "upper crust" Hawkes Bay family to become a nurse in Christchurch and then marry a man of no means who wanted to be a farmer.

Her father responded by cutting her off from the family. He made her an outcast who would have to fend for herself from then on.

The Robilliards learned about farming by labouring on a sheep station at Waipara, in North Canterbury. Desperate to get their own place, they found at last a steep, rocky and weed-infested block near Takaka, in Golden Bay. It was for sale but was in such a poor state that land agents had given up showing it to prospective buyers. A succession of previous owners had walked off the place. It was a no-hoper.

So, of course, in the 1950s, the Robilliards bought it. With young children, a hefty mortgage and the pitying looks of neighbours, they set about rebuilding the derelict house and sheds, taming the land, straining wire fences and tending stock that seemed determined not to thrive.

Chatting over coffee, Robbie admits: "We were on our absolute knees, grovelling in poverty". Unpaid bills, some with "final demand" stamped on them, were piling up on the wooden box they used for a kitchen table. The children were heading to school in clothes

Robbie had sewed from old flour bags.

For Garry, there seemed no way out but he would never surrender. He just worked himself ever harder.

For Robbie, though, there had to be a way and she found it in her gift for words. She began writing articles about country life and submitting them to newspapers and magazines. They were accepted and published. Then editors started approaching her for more. Next came an offer that astounded her. Would she tour the world and send back stories of life in other countries? Would she what!

The penniless farmer became a roving writer. She built up a considerable following with her dispatches from many countries. She was bold enough to visit and write about North Korea, where bitterness from the Korean War still simmered, and Eastern European countries where revolt was simmering against Soviet hegemony behind the Iron Curtain. Down on the farm the cheques rolled in and Garry found time between farming tasks to pay the bills.

An earlier indication of Robbie's spirit was in her "whistle-blowing" while working at a Golden Bay geriatric hospital. Her training and experience in nursing had helped her get the job. They also highlighted for her the

Below: Hard country, hard life, soft woman: Robin Robilliard survived a tough existence to remain ever cheerful and considerate of others. The Takaka farmer wrote the story of her life in *Hard Country*. Readers warmed to her gifted story telling and her amazing range of experiences.

"cruel" treatment of patients there. Appalled by this she complained to the management. She was brushed off so she went higher, to the Nelson health authorities. They also took no action. The management then fired her.

The Robilliards, an indomitable couple in disparate ways, persevered on the hill-country farm for 57 years and made it profitable.

Not too far away, in Golden Bay, Lorna Langford was running her quaint general store and making it into a heritage attraction simply by changing nothing.

I had visited the Bainham Store, up the Aorere River from Collingwood, in Golden Bay, on holiday in the 1980s. Owner and operator Langford had impressed me then as a special sort of person with huge regard for history. In 2007 I go back to interview her for a Heartland column.

One of New Zealand's earliest gold rushes occurred around Bainham in the 1850s. It is no wonder, then, that several stores opened to serve gold diggers, sawmill workers and farmers.

Langford's store and post office are the only businesses that remain in this lush dairy farming valley. The present store is not the original one but it is old. And, in 2007, it is virtually unchanged – a veritable living museum.

Above: Bainham storekeeper Lorna Langford made few concessions to trends and fashions. The store she ran for more than half a century changed little, although, as she said, it still had to turn a profit. And it did, thanks to local farmers, trampers and holidaymakers who supported it.

Below: Step back in time, through the door of Langford's Store at Bainham, inland from Collingwood. Lorna Langford took over the store from her father and ran it for more than half a century as a working museum. Her niece Sukhita, and her husband Will Hutchison, maintain the tradition.

Behind the counter I find Langford seemingly unchanged. Her hair is a little whiter but her eyes are still sparkling blue. Though in her 80s, her sprightliness belies her 53 years experience of running the business.

Her grandfather ran it through the Depression years of the 1930s when a stream of unemployed men drifted into Bainham to fossick for any gold that the earlier prospectors had missed. Her grandfather registered as a gold buyer. He recorded his transactions in a book that is now a valued museum exhibit.

Langford started working for her grandfather at the store in 1947. She graduated to postmistress in 1952 and became proprietor in 1954.

A trickle of customers enters the shop while I am there. Langford enjoys talking to all, local farm people as much as trampers on their way to the Heaphy Track. While they chat, I take time to notice the variety of goods in this Aladdin's Cave where items are still packed on shelves behind the counter, unlike a modern supermarket.

Old labels and faded signs mingle with modern products. This is very much a working shop.

"I need to keep selling," Langford says.

She needs people's feet to keep treading on the wooden doorstep that has been worn into a glacial valley shape by decades of boots and shoes.

How long can she go on, I ask? She smiles and, half-closing her eyes in conspiratorial gesture, says she has been training a niece to take over. She will be retiring soon.

Later I mention to a *Nelson Evening Mail* reporter that she should keep a check on Langford because her retirement will be a good story. The reporter laughs and says Langford has been talking retirement for years. It will never happen, she adds.

Oh well, at least I tried. A month later, the changeover at the Bainham Store is in the news.

EBENEZER TEICHELMANN IS A name to marvel at but not one you would expect to find in the bawdy goldfields town of Hokitika.

However, it was in Hokitika in 2009 that I come upon the story of the man known and admired by all as "The Little Doctor".

Brian Ward tells me about him. And Ward should know, for he and partner Frances Flanagan own and run the bed and breakfast in the building that was Teichelmann's house, surgery and private convalescent hospital in the early 1900s.

Ward played the part of Teichelmann in the pageant celebrating the Hokitika library's centennial in 2008. The Little Doctor had done much to secure funding for the library (now the Hokitika Museum) from American philanthropist Andrew Carnegie.

Playing the role of Teichelmann has made Ward a devoted fan of the historic figure. He and Flanagan restored the B&B and made it a veritable shrine to the man who had done so much for Hokitika. Memorabilia of the doctor are spread through the house. The items arouse much interest among guests, Ward says.

Teichelmann's wife died young and he had no children. So he dedicated himself to the health care of the Westland community. He made house calls at all hours and over all parts of the sprawling region. He saw patients in

Below: A long-deceased Hokitika doctor is remembered in his former home. Brian Ward (left) bought the building that housed Dr Ebenezer Teichelmann's surgery, hospital and residence, and converted it to a bed and breakfast establishment. After reading of Teichelmann's dedication to West Coasters' health and his mountaineering exploits, Ward made the place a shrine to the diminutive man who was known and loved as "The Little Doctor".

the general practice clinic at his home. He did operations at the small hospital he developed at home and at Westland Hospital, of which he was the medical superintendent.

When World War I broke out Teichelmann answered the call and served as a medical officer with New Zealand troops overseas. He was aboard the transport ship Marquette when it was sunk by a German submarine in the Mediterranean Sea in 1915. He survived the disaster in which 10 New Zealand nurses perished when the ship went down.

Teichelmann was also an accomplished mountaineer. He climbed numerous alpine peaks and glaciers. He was in the climbing party that completed the third ascent of Aoraki, Mt Cook. He took to aviation with enthusiasm and made some of the earliest flights over South Westland, as a passenger.

The Little Doctor, who stood only 1.64 metres tall (about 5 feet, 4 inches), died in 1938. A memorial seat to Teichelmann stands outside the museum, opposite his former home.

A FREQUENT TRAVELLER passing through Kumara cannot help remarking on the change in this town over the last few years. The old gold town on the Arthurs Pass highway seemed in terminal decay a decade ago. Now it is looking spruce and progressive.

In 2014 I meet Kerrie Fitzgibbon in Kumara's Theatre Royal Hotel. Of this human dynamo it could be said: she came, she saw, she conquered.

Fitzgibbon hailed from a farm near Riverton in Southland. Her family moved to Christchurch when she was 12. On a trip to the West Coast a few years after, she felt a special tug on her heart strings in Kumara. It was enough to draw her back again and again. Husband Mark and their children built a bach there in 1970 and she started staying for longer and longer spells. Finally, she gave up her

hairdressing business in Christchurch and moved permanently to Kumara.

Stories about the old buildings and gold workings stirred an interest in history. She began voluntary work at the Hokitika museum, which gave her ready access to historical items and time to study them.

Sure of the support of her husband and family, Fitzgibbon bought the Theatre Royal Hotel and brought it back to its golden glory days. She bought and renovated several other properties to provide added accommodation options for visitors.

And visitors started coming. The new cycle trail between Hokitika and Greymouth, via back roads and tracks, has delivered a succession of riders, runners and walkers to her door seeking meals and beds.

Fitzgibbon's shrewd business sense had anticipated this when the cycle trail was just a proposal. She had a vision of bunches of tired, thirsty callers and of what she could offer to make them stay a while.

"We had to be able to feed them, bed them, lubricate them and entertain them," she says.

Part of the entertainment is live music but equally important is the presentation of historic tales of Kumara on large billboards around the town.

"I believe," Fitzgibbon says, "the future is in the past".

ANDRIS APSE WAS A REFUGEE from war-torn Latvia. He found peace at Okarito.

Enchanted by his magnificent landscape photographs, I arrange in 2014 to visit him in his hillside eyrie with its panoramic view of the Tasman Sea. From his wide windows the changing moods of storm, spume and spray and the golden sunsets are spellbinding.

Okarito is more than just another former gold town. The road to the village winds through ancient bush, from the South

Left: Andris Apse shares the stories of natural beauty, in pictures that tell a thousand words. The former Latvian refugee is a leading landscape photographer. From his home above the beach at Okarito, near Franz Josef Glacier, he "roughs it" in bush and on mountain slopes to capture images just as he wants them.

Westland highway, halfway between Franz Josef and Whataroa. Beside the road are warning signs that I have never found elsewhere – they urge care not to run over wandering kiwi. In tall trees along the river and lagoon the stately kotuku (white heron) nest.

You can count permanent residents on your fingers and toes but their numbers are swelled by bach owners and holidaymakers. At the pioneer-era Donovan's Store, which is now a community centre, you are as likely to catch a classical trio playing dreamy Schubert melodies, as a stand-up comedian in scurrilous full cry. While down on the beach you may find groups of newly found friends socialising around a driftwood bonfire. You may hear them marvel at the sight of the sun's last rays fading from the peak of Aoraki, Mt Cook, in the east and view the glory of clouds ablaze with reds and golds as the orb slips beneath the Tasman horizon to the west.

All this was part of the reason for Apse settling here with partner Lynne and their children. Apse breathes the magic of land, sea and sky and hungers to capture it in his camera. He is a true outdoors man who can, and often does, live for days on end in the bush, seeking images for his art.

The images, printed, framed and hung in galleries at his home and in Franz Josef, sell for handsome prices. Many are reproduced in books and on calendars. They ensure a lifestyle he could only have dreamed of in Latvia.

Soon after Apse was born, in 1943, his father was dragooned to fight for the Germans against the Russians in World War II. The father was not seen again. Inquiries found nothing and he was presumed dead. The infant Apse and his mother drifted with streams of fellow refugees, from town to town, camp to camp. At last, in 1949, they sailed to New Zealand.

Apse started as a professional photographer in Canterbury, doing everything from weddings to school portraits. But his heart was always in landscape and, as soon as he could make a living from it, he took it up full-time. The shift to Okarito followed family camping holidays there, during which he fell in love with the place.

As he talks about his solo treks on remote beaches, in primeval bush and through forgotten gold mining claims, I begin to think of him as a loner. But then he mentions his involvement with Okarito's community association which earns revenue from contracts with the local council for pest eradication, reserve maintenance and camping ground management. The money goes towards enhancing the township and restoring its heritage features, such as Donovan's store.

A DIFFERENT SORT OF ARTIST is Brian Turner. He is a poet whose work I can understand, not only because he writes in plain language but also because he writes of places familiar to me, Otago's Maniototo District, where I lived from 1974 to 1977.

Turner moved from Dunedin to Oturehua in the late 1990s. He describes his shift as part of a widespread "flight from the cities" but hints also at relationship problems.

"I like this country a lot," he says. "The harsh climate is a challenge but it has something of the cleanest air on the planet. The subtle colours in the landscape are just enchanting, the shadows in the valleys, the shapes of the clouds when the wind blows."

Doesn't it sound like Andris Apse? The two are in raptures about the character and beauty of their respective areas. Each has an element of loner about him. But Turner is a singular personality. People may think him gruff and a trifle crusty. I doubt if he minds what they think of him.

The morning I arrive in 2008 he is loading his wheelbarrow with firewood for his log burner in this place where ponds freeze hard enough to skate on, where hoar frosts drizzle tree branches with stalactites, where striking permafrost would shatter a shovel. He invites me in and puts the kettle on. He has the Concert Programme playing on the radio.

I had met him a few years before and he seems happy to see me back. We talk mainly of his views on landscape conservation, centred on a campaign opposing the erection of wind turbines on Maniototo's rock-strewn ranges. He tells me of his fishing and cycling in the area and the inspiration he gets from the environment for his writing.

Turner remembers his youth as a time of waiting for weekends so he could get away from the city and into the wilds of Central Otago. Now he has made it permanently.

He makes the point that reforming types used to say New Zealand closed down at weekends but he believes it opened up at weekends, as city folk were released to head into the wide open spaces.

That hardly sounds gruff and crusty. But I recall, before my previous visit, that my editor asked me to go down and interview him for a feature. The editor had already written to him asking if he would agree to my coming and adding that I was a fan of his poetry.

Turner's curt reply came in six words: "Send the adoring bugger down then". Yes, I understand his language.

Left: It could be the Oturehua library but no; this is Brian Turner at home with his books. The environmentalist, angler, cyclist, poet and sportsman chose tiny Oturehua, in Central Otago, as a base where he could get away from the madding crowd and live as one with nature.

Opposite: The Haast River Bridge was in the headlines when the body of British hitchhiker Jennifer Beard was found beneath it in 1969. Her murder remains unsolved. The bridge is a link on the highway between Hokitika and Haast that continues over Haast Pass to Central Otago on the South Island's Great Circle tourist route.

It is an unwritten law that people who live in Haast must love the place.

Betty Eggeling has lived there since arriving as a child in 1930. She has kept the law of loving this separate world at the end of the road down the West Coast. It has not always been easy in this realm of the three Rs: rain, remoteness and rivers. But at least she has not had to put up with that dreaded double-R, rat race.

She tells me in 2005 how her memories of Haast can be classified in two chapters. There are the years before the road went through and the years after it was completed.

In the early stage, contact with the world was by an air link with Hokitika. The plane landed daily on the driest strip of grass south of the glaciers. It brought bread and *The Press*, which had arrived earlier that day at Hokitika by railcar from Christchurch. It loaded whitebait from the local canning factory and other produce of the district. It carried passengers, too, including Eggeling's sons who went to boarding school in Christchurch.

Eggeling worked with her husband on the farm. She rode the legendary cattle drive on horseback to the Whataroa saleyards each March. The 10-day drive included horses and cattle sometimes fording and sometimes swimming across treacherous rivers, she says.

The Haast Pass highway was completed in 1965, though three decades would pass before it was sealed the whole way. Oh what a difference it made, says Eggeling. Haast residents could now drive to Wanaka more quickly and easily than they could to Hokitika.

The biggest change was in tourism. Visitor numbers rose as coaches, cars and caravans tackled the grand circle route from Christchurch to Hokitika, through the Haast and on to Queenstown before returning to Christchurch.

Eggeling and her husband saw the potential in tourism and established a motor camp. It was a giant step for a couple who had known little of the outside world and even less of business other than farming. But it was successful and provided steady income to supplement their farming earnings.

I am not surprised the camp became popular with travellers. Eggeling's friendliness and patience would have made visitors feel most welcome.

These are just a few of many people I interviewed on Heartland travels. One thing they have in common is absolute absence of any feeling of self-importance. They would insist they are ordinary folk.

Often on my travels I meet extraordinary folk, though not always at first-hand. Some of the tales are told to me by country people proud of the deeds of their forebears.

My editor once suggested I find some residents at the top of the Takaka Hill to interview. Knowing the barren summit of Takaka Hill, I am half sure he is pulling my leg. But, just in case, I drive up there.

The road is a seemingly endless upward spiral through curves that give you giddying views of the land far below. Nearing the top I notice a sign pointing to a farm stay. Then, as I reach the top, I see the marble quarry.

Suddenly it hits me. Jim Henderson wrote a book on his early life, called *Down from Marble Mountain*. I know Henderson came from somewhere around here because I wrote his obituary for *The Press*. Could it be …?

I double back to the farm stay sign and take the drive to the homestead. There I meet a tall, tanned farmer pulling on his work boots after finishing lunch. I ask him if this could be where Jim Henderson used to live. He confirms it and adds that he is Henderson's nephew. I tell him I wrote Henderson's obituary for *The Press* a couple of weeks ago and he slips his boots off again.

"Come in," he says. With typical country courtesy he offers tea and gives up an hour to chat about his uncle and show me photographs of the farmer, World War II soldier, author and broadcaster who was a popular figure in New Zealand through the 1950s and 1960s.

A sign in Gaelic on a stone cairn marks the place where history's most famous sheep rustler was caught. The memorial to James Mackenzie stands on a barren and windblown hill at the eastern edge of the Mackenzie Country. The road over this hill is known as the Mackenzie Pass.

I take the easy drive up and over the pass in 2010, starting at Albury. As the road climbs it changes from tarseal to shingle and the landscape switches from grassy paddocks to tussock and matagouri. Reaching the cairn, I find it is three-sided, with inscriptions in English and Maori as well as Gaelic. The English version reads: "On this spot James Mackenzie the free-booter was captured by John Sidebottom and the Maoris Taiko and Seventeen and escaped from them the same night, 4 March, 1855".

Mackenzie was an immigrant shepherd from Scotland who, it is said, could speak only Gaelic. He is thought to have been the first European to use this pass.

Up here, the story goes, he drove sheep he had stolen from The Levels station, near Timaru. Legend has it he was intending to drive the sheep over the Lindis Pass as well, and all the way to Southland where he would sell them to unsuspecting buyers.

Also according to legend, he had slit his dog's tongue so it could not bark and no one would hear him moving the sheep.

When someone becomes a folk hero, facts are often embellished. What is known is that Mackenzie was tracked to this lonely spot on the hill by Sidebottom, Taiko and Seventeen. He escaped was recaptured, escaped again and was captured again. He was jailed but, guess what? He escaped again. But once more he was recaptured.

After several months in Lyttelton Jail, Mackenzie was pardoned on grounds that he had been badly treated. He then left the country.

Opposite: It could be a statue of The Good Shepherd. But this shepherd was, according to legend, bad. Scotsman James Mackenzie was said to have stolen a large mob of sheep from a South Canterbury station. The story of his sheep handling, capture and trial made him a folk hero. His statue, by Sam Mahon, stands in the main street of Fairlie.

I leave the cairn and drive down the hill to the wide basin of the Mackenzie Country, turn right at Dog Kennel Corner and emerge on State Highway 8. From there it is a short climb to Burkes Pass, then on to Fairlie.

A sculpture of Mackenzie and his dog stands in the main street of Fairlie. The life-size representation of a wily shepherd and his efficient dog seems to capture the romance of the Mackenzie legend. It suggests the sheep stealer is more popular around here now than he was 160 years ago.

OF COURSE, CATRIONA BAKER could never have met Mackenzie in real life. But when we chat in her room at a Fairlie rest home in 2013, I almost get the feeling they are old mates.

Bedridden as she approaches 100 years, Baker talks with great clarity about station life in the Mackenzie Country. She claims her research, her experience in sheep work and her grandfather's reminiscences have given her an understanding of the Scottish shepherd and an empathy with him. With co-writer Linda Sundberg she has produced a book on Mackenzie that challenges the orthodox histories.

Baker is in awe of Mackenzie's talent as a stockman. She says he was well grounded in sheep work back home in the Scottish Highlands. If he was a sheep stealer, he might have learned that art there too, as rustling was rife in the years of harsh clan rivalries. However, he came to New Zealand intending to buy land and farm on his own account. His inability to communicate in English must have hampered him in this ambition, she says.

Never mind Mackenzie, though. Baker is a character of note too. With wit and passion she tells me of mustering merinos on horseback up the Tasman River against the backdrop of majestic Mt Cook. With a team of musterers and their packs of dogs, she used to drive the sheep from Balmoral Station, which she owned, to the yards and shearing shed at Mt Cook Station, owned by her brother, Donald Burnett.

This muster was done twice a year, each way, for dipping and shearing, Baker says. In 20 years, from 1953 to 1973, she missed taking part only twice.

Baker and Burnett ran the two stations together. Their grandfather, Andrew Burnett, established Mt Cook Station and it stayed in the family's hands for a century and a half. His son, Thomas Burnett, ran the station while serving also as a Member of Parliament. Donald took it over and Thomas bought Balmoral for his daughter so the siblings could each have a station.

Her grandfather was mixing with other South Canterbury runholders in the years that Mackenzie was active in the area and being reported in the newspapers. Mackenzie was a topic of many conversations among the men, Baker says.

Being an adept horsewoman and dog handler, and expert at managing mobs of sheep, Baker was accepted by the rugged types who moved from station to station for the mustering or the shearing. She relishes telling tales about them, such as the one about the shearers celebrating after "cutting out" (completing the shearing) at the Mt Cook shed. The men would take their pay cheques to the pub at Tekapo and pin them on the wall of the bar. These hard cases would then continue drinking until the money was all gone. While the publican pocketed the cheques, the shearers would stagger outside and slump on a wooden bench to endure their hangovers.

That bench became known as The Penitents' Form, Baker laughs. Her father souvenired it and it became an honoured piece of furniture at Mt Cook Station.

ANOTHER MAN ASSOCIATED with a mountain pass is Arthur Dobson. The pass he found is named after him, not as Dobsons Pass, but Arthurs Pass. Using his surname would have been confusing as his father and two brothers were also seeking a new way through the Southern Alps.

Arthur had heard of the pass from Maori who told him warring parties had used it in past generations. Yet, when he found it, his first reaction to it was negative because of its steepness.

John Charles, a stalwart of Arthurs Pass Village, has been heavily involved in developing a walking track along the route which Arthur is thought to have been taking when he found the pass in 1864. The track was opened in 2014 to mark the 150th anniversary of the discovery.

A year before this, Charles, local historian John Wilson, and Department of Conservation senior ranger Chris Stewart guide me on the track and tell me about their research into Dobson. They have found he gained a surveying contract on the West Coast and needed to make frequent trips there. Other passes were too far away so he decided to look for the ancient Maori one.

Above: Traffic heading to the West Coast grinds up to the summit of Arthurs Pass, marked by the memorial to Arthur Dobson. The explorer and surveyor had heard of the pass from Maori but, on first sight, judged it unsuitable for a road. However, on second sight, and after traversing the steep Otira section, he proposed it for the principal route from Christchurch to Hokitika.

He and brother Edward found the pass but, looking down to the Otira side, judged it too steep for horses to negotiate. They turned back and arrived at Francis Goldney's station, near Cass. Goldney was interested in their story as he wanted more grazing land. He persuaded Arthur Dobson and a shepherd to accompany him back to the pass.

The small party left their horses above the Bealey River and hacked their way to the top of the pass. There they lowered a dog in a sling, then made the difficult descent. Thus they were the first Europeans to cross Arthurs Pass.

In two days of searching the men found no ground on the Otira side suitable for grazing. Giving up their quest, they climbed back up the pass. They reached Goldney's station almost a week after setting out.

But that was not to be the end of Arthurs Pass. Just four months later, gold was discovered in Westland and a fast route from Christchurch to the diggings became a priority for the Canterbury Provincial Council.

Arthur's pass was confirmed as the best option and a track was quickly formed there. Within months it was upgraded to a road. By mid-1866 regular coach services were using Arthurs Pass.

What did Dobson think of all this? Perhaps he was too busy to say. For he served as an explorer, surveyor and engineer in the Nelson and Buller areas for many years before returning to Christchurch, where he was City Engineer for 20 years. He died in 1934, aged 92.

Not much is known of Mick Stimpson. However, he does share one mark of significance with William O'Leary. Both old-timers were immortalised in poetry by Christchurch writer Denis Glover.

I come across Stimpson's story while visiting Port Levy, on Banks Peninsula, in 2007. In the Maori cemetery on the hill above the settlement I find the grave of this Irish seaman.

Stimpson deserted from his Royal Navy ship and ran away to live among the Maori early last century. He felt at home in Port Levy and became a respected figure there, popular for his stories of the sea and helpful with his predictions for weather and good fishing spots.

I meet Jack and Sylvia Coxon at Port Levy in 2007. They knew Stimpson and remember him well. They say the Maori community took him in and sheltered him from any chance of capture and arrest.

A local Maori chief gave Stimpson a shack to live in, the Coxons say. It stood on the section where they now live but it was demolished long ago. They remember Stimpson inviting them in for a cuppa sometime in the 1930s.

The old sailor had a bowl of water boiling over the fire. He poured it into a pot, tossed in a handful of tea leaves and stirred it. Then he took a swig himself, before passing it to each of the Coxons in turn. He never used cups, they say.

It was not tea, but stories, that made Stimpson special, the Coxons say. People, especially children, used to gather round to hear his yarns. Which is probably how Glover found and came to revere him. The poet once referred to Stimpson as his mentor. He dedicated to him his last major work, *Towards Banks Peninsula*.

When Stimpson died, in 1946, Glover wrote a further dedication in verse. It is inscribed on Stimpson's headstone:

"You were these hills and the sea./ In calm, or the winter wave and snow./ Lie then peaceful among them./ The hills iron, the quiet tides below".

William O'Leary is better known by the name Arawata Bill. This is also the title Glover gave to a poem about him, written in 1953, six years after O'Leary's death at 82.

I cross the Arawata River on the way to Jackson Bay, below Haast, in 2011. I slow down and peer upriver. Beyond the shingle banks, below the cloven hills and through the mist I see the ghostly figure of an old man in a three-piece suit leading a heavily laden pack horse onto the grassy river terrace.

That is pure fancy, of course, but this is the kind of fascination O'Leary has inspired in ordinary people for more than half a century.

O'Leary was, and preferred to be, a man alone. Ever optimistic of finding gold in South Westland's hills, he trekked there each year from Glenorchy, at the head of Lake Wakatipu, over almost impenetrable mountains, and remained ever the gentleman.

Perhaps more than anything, it is the pathos in accounts of his declining years that drives the nostalgia I feel for him. Even in old age and infirmity, O'Leary still believed that gold was there waiting for him. He still wanted to go back for it. He still gazed at those mountains wistfully.

The image of O'Leary, escaped from his Dunedin rest home and heading out on the Queenstown road by foot, strikes at the heart of anyone raised in the New Zealand ethos of man-alone.

Below: Mick Stimpson's grave commands a view of Port Levy, Banks Peninsula, that has hardly changed since his time. The sailor deserted his Royal Navy ship and was sheltered by local Maori. He became a popular storyteller and forecaster of weather and fishing patterns. He was immortalised in a poem by Denis Glover.

CHAPTER 6

Further up Central

A FRENZY OF GOLD DIGGING left two prospectors near starvation point. They had struck it rich in Central Otago in the 1860s. They knew other diggers might find them at any moment, so they worked on and on without thinking of a trip to replenish food supplies.

They were surviving on a diet of dry bread. When their story became known, the area where they had made their lucky strike was named Drybread.

Goldfields attracted such unusual names. Good stories often lurk behind them. Sometimes conflicting stories were told and you wouldn't know which one to believe.

I used to wonder how the long-lost gold town of Drybread, up the Manuherikia Valley north of Alexandra, got its name. When I visit in 2013, Karen Glassford solves the puzzle. Her version of the story, admittedly one of several, seems the most likely. After all, the former gold diggers' settlement is on the Glassford family farm. Motivated by this, she has done some thorough research into the matter.

Glassford tells the story of the two prospectors who arrived in the area, leading a nanny goat on a rope and humping a sack of bread for their sustenance. They pitched a tent and poked around the creeks and gullies digging exploratory holes. Then they struck it rich.

The men returned to their camp each evening, milked the goat, soaked some of the stale bread in the warm milk and ate their simple meal. One day, however, they found the goat had gone dry.

Would they pack their up their gold, head to the nearest town and buy a slap-up meal? Or would they stay here, keep on digging and clean out the rich vein of gold before nosey latecomers drifted over the hill and spotted them?

They chose the latter course and worked on. They ate their bread dry until it ran out and hunger forced them to leave.

Word got out, as it always did on the goldfields, and soon a troop of diggers was picking and shovelling at Drybread. Then the sluicing companies moved in.

Hardly anything remains to show they were ever there. The most obvious sign is a small cemetery. Glassford says some burials were made informally before the cemetery was properly established in 1870 by a mining company manager whose young son had died.

Glassford found the boy's overgrown grave by chance while chopping out thistles. The inscription showed it was the grave of Thomas Greenbank, aged 20 months. Cemetery

Opposite: Prospectors trudged the Old Dunstan Trail, over the Central Otago highlands to the goldfields. Now known as the Old Dunstan Road, its condition is improved but it is recommended as a summer road for 4WD vehicles. It runs from Clarks Junction in the east to Moa Creek in the west.

Above: Karen Glassford is on a mission. The Central Otago farmer was dismayed at the state of the historic cemetery at Drybread and launched community efforts to tidy it up. Many working bees later, and with help from local businesses, the cemetery has come alive again. Glassford's research has revealed some interesting stories that had been buried there.

Below: Tricia Batkin descends from the pioneering Harley family in the Lauder-Becks area of Central Otago. The road ahead leads to St Bathans, the road at left to Cambrian. The latter was once known as Welshman's Gully because of the predominance of Welsh gold miners there. With St Bathans dominated by Irish diggers, rivalry occasionally broke out into scuffles, she says.

documents listed his as the first recorded burial here.

The cemetery is on a sloping paddock behind a belt of trees, hidden from the road, a few kilometres north-west of Omakau.

Glassford and neighbouring farmer Ross Naylor have recently led community efforts to tidy up the cemetery, repair broken graves and erect a fence around it to keep stock out.

For Naylor, the work is emotional and satisfying. He is the fifth of six generations of his family to farm at Drybread. Two of his great-great-grandfathers rest in this cemetery. He has his plot secured here too.

You don't have to travel far from Drybread to find other old gold towns quaintly named. Just up the road is Matakanui. During the gold rush it was known as Tinkers. It is said this name related to some metalworkers who carried on their trade here, mending gold pans, picks, shovels, billies and pots.

Miners from all over the Manuherikia diggings trekked to Tinkers to get their gear repaired. Glassford says a shrewd publican opened a bar beside the road to Drybread and called it the Matakanui Welcome Inn. Unknowing diggers arriving there and thinking they had reached Tinkers, were eager to step inside for some liquor. Many of them never made it to the real Tinkers.

North of Drybread is Cambrian, or Cambrians, depending on whether you are of Welsh ancestry. Welsh diggers congregated here and established such an enclave that the settlement became known as Welshman's Gully. That's a long name to fit on a road sign, hence the change. But the Welsh connection was retained, as Cambria was the old Roman name for Wales.

Coal also was found in the lower reaches of the Dunstan Range, behind Cambrian. Some of the gold diggers had been coal miners in Wales. The fuel they provided meant the village people did not suffer as much from bitter winters as others in Central Otago did.

A dozen houses line the road up the gully at Cambrian. In one of them lives artist Grahame Sydney. The former Dunedin man tells me in 2014 how much he loves this place. He says the world outside his front window is "a daily cinema and I have the best seat in the house".

The window is his screen; Cambrian is the movie. Scenes of light playing on mountain snow, changing shadows, hues and shades, soaring hawks and wispy clouds are the characters that absorb his observation and imagination.

In another house lives Tricia Batkin. She is from the Harley family of Cambrian pioneers.

Opposite Batkin's house a tiny cemetery sits on a small knoll. The local Cambrian-St Bathans Rural Women's Group has recently tidied the cemetery and erected a plaque and an interpretation panel here. Batkin led the research for this project. It turned up information that was new to her but it also raised some questions, she says.

The land set aside for the cemetery was once more expansive. But when the big sluicing companies moved in to carve away hillsides for the precious gold, much of the cemetery plot had to go. The bit that was left, now surrounded by a white picket fence, is about the size of a small house. Seven graves were dug up and the human remains transferred to the St Bathans cemetery, about four kilometres away.

Batkin unearthed the names of the bodies that were exhumed. A few were miners killed in accidents. One was a boy aged 1 year. One was Mary Rothwell, 23, who drowned attempting to cross the Manuherikia River while on the 60-kilometre walk from Clyde to Hills Creek where she hoped to get a job as a hotel maid.

Three graves remain undisturbed at Cambrian. Batkin has identified one as the grave of a man killed when his loaded dray capsized. A second may contain the bones of a miner who was accidentally shot. And the third? That is a mystery, she says.

The wooden headstone of the third grave, broken into several pieces, is badly weather-worn and the writing on it is illegible. Batkin consulted an old timer who said that headstone had puzzled everyone as long as he could remember. So, one of the departed of Cambrian is gone … and forgotten.

This saddens Batkin but she smiles again as she talks about relations between the neighbouring gold towns of Cambrian and St Bathans. Irish miners descended upon St Bathans, which became a bastion of Catholicism. The Welsh miners of Cambrian were Methodist. Rivalry between the two was said to be fierce at times. It broke out in scuffles and fights which some locals laughed off as "The Wars of the Roses".

The combined women's group may be witness to a more enlightened view of religious differences. If so, the seven Cambrian departed should be able to rest in peace among the graves of the St Bathans' dead.

St Bathans is one of only two goldfield towns in the Manuherikia Valley to have survived as a living village. It is much smaller than in its heyday but the Vulcan Hotel is still open, two churches are still used, a clutch of residents live here and a few heritage buildings remain.

This so nearly did not happen. Sluicing operations that created a lake where a hill had stood, opposite the hotel, put the town in danger of collapse. Mining was ordered to stop, for the preservation of St Bathans – and it did.

The hill at St Bathans was called Kildare Hill. That's the Irish connection again. The lake was named Blue Lake. Its water once was blue but had turned to green when I lived close by in the 1970s. With the white sculpted cliffs around it, the lake is a visitor attraction.

Another attraction is the ghost of the Vulcan Hotel. A myth grew up that the ghost of a woman who died in the front-corner bedroom haunts the hotel. That might be enough to draw a few visitors but a triathlon that started and finished outside that window was a bigger attraction for St Bathans.

Local farmer Don Harley (Trish Batkin's brother) initiated the race and gave it the title Ghost to Ghost. Harley, once a supremely fit Otago rugby flanker, takes me around the course, which includes a kayak stage on Blue Lake, in his 4WD.

That was nearly 20 years ago. More recently Grahame Sydney captured a photographic image of Harley propped up by a cushion as he slumps on a chair in a farm shed. Behind the hard man of Cambrian, all is shadow. Before him, an open door lets the sun pour in to light his face. Soon after, Harley died from motor-neuron disease.

Other Manuherikia gold towns include Ophir, named after a fabulously rich African city in classical times, and Vinegar Hill, named after the site of a battle between Irish rebels and British troops in the 1798 uprising.

Two diggers discovered gold at Vinegar Hill, near Cambrian. They covered their traces carefully so others would not find the claim. It was later said that if others heard about this subterfuge, there would have been a riot on the scale of the old Irish-British fight.

There were many more gold towns in Otago. Some have gone, some still exist. Romantic names roll off the tongue like an honours list: Arrowtown, Bannockburn, Bendigo, Cardrona, Hamilton, Kyeburn, Naseby, Macetown, Skippers, Waitahuna and more.

Gold was discovered also in Southland and North Otago. These are separate regions now but were all part of Otago in the provincial era of New Zealand history.

Below: If it's heritage buildings you want to see, go to Ophir. The centre of a rich goldfield, north of Alexandra, lost its lustre when the Otago Central railway bypassed it and boosted neighbouring Omakau instead. The solid stone buildings remained intact and are an attraction for travellers.

Well into the 21st century the digging still goes on. Mining companies are working at some fields, such as Moa Creek, at the head of the Ida Valley. This was once an accommodation stop for diggers trekking the Old Dunstan Trail over the hills to Central Otago, not to be confused with Moa Flat near Heriot. Then there is the giant opencast mine at Macraes Flat.

Margaret Leaker tells me about school holidays at Macraes in the 1950s, when her father worked there. He later worked on roading projects around Otago but returned to Macraes after he retired, to fossick for gold. Winter on the high plateau inland from Palmerston was too hard on his health, though, and he had to give it up.

When Leaker sees the giant diggers chewing the land at Macraes in the modern era, she fancies she can hear her father say with a chuckle: "I always knew the gold was there".

Gold was found in many places. In Southland, north-west of Gore, was the Switzers goldfield, near the present town of Waikaia. I go there in 2013 and learn that Switzer was an early German settler. Gold was found in 1861 and a series of rushes followed. As at St Bathans, the workings threatened to undermine the township of Waikaia. Unlike St Bathans, the mining did not stop. Instead, Waikaia was shifted – twice. Now that's pragmatism.

Sixteen pubs served the diggers at Waikaia in the days when the King Solomon Mine prospered. A dozen dredges operated in the Waikaia River. Mining continued until World War II. It is hard now to imagine all this activity in and around such an attractive town that services a district of well-ordered farms.

If Waikaia sounds more like a part of Central Otago than of Southland, then resident Alvin Ashby is not surprised. Waikaia's sheltered valley enjoys a Central Otago climate, he says.

"The difference between here and Gore is unreal. It can be teeming in Invercargill but very dry here," Ashby says.

I arrange to meet Ashby in the Waikaia pub in 2013. He tells me he moved here from Gore when he retired. He spends much of his time fishing and finds the rivers around here ideal for trout. Ah, so that explains why, to my surprise, the motels were nearly booked out.

In North Otago, deep in the hills above the Waitaki River, I find the near-ghost town of Livingstone, in 2012. Here I visit local farmer John McKenzie. He has studied the area's history and gives talks to visiting groups. He says gold was discovered here in 1863 and a substantial town grew up to support the diggers. Mining petered out from the late 1870s and the town slowly declined.

But there is more to it than that. McKenzie says mining began and was carried on for seven years before it became legal. It was common for prospectors to start digging as soon as they found gold, rather than have it advertised too widely, too soon. They would register their claim some time later. However, seven years seems a long time to operate without a licence.

The first known public reference to gold mining at the Livingstone and Maerewhenua fields appeared in a newspaper in 1868. It was not until the following year that a goldfields warden appeared on the scene to see what was going on. He had ridden his horse over the Dansey Pass from Naseby, which would have been at least a full-day's trip.

Apparently the warden was not too concerned to find a group of diggers hard at work. After checking that everything was going satisfactorily, he rode back to Naseby. Back home he prepared the necessary certificates that declared the Livingstone-Maerewhenua area officially a goldfield.

The North Otago hills get very dry in summer, so water was a problem. McKenzie says

up to 80 men laboured to build dams and races to bring water up to 40 kilometres to the sluice guns at the battle front.

A decade later, nearly all activity ended, as gold returns diminished. However, the Depression of the 1930s brought new diggers into the area. Hopes were high and 70 men were taken on to dig out and repair the old water races. Money was so short that they were paid in food and tobacco, McKenzie says.

As the economy picked up and men started going away to fight in World War II, mining stopped again. No substantial mining was done here again.

Signs of the gold diggings remain in carved cliffs and rumpled gullies where the sluice guns reduced hills to piles of silt now over-grown with gorse and scrub.

Every gold town turned up colourful char-acters. McKenzie tells me of a man who worked on the diggings all day and ran a bar for thirsty miners in the evenings. His pub opening hours breached the law of six-o'clock closing of all liquor outlets. Police raided his bar regularly and he was fined each time. Asked to explain his behaviour, he complained that he had to keep up his mining to pay his court fines so, of course, he couldn't run a bar in the daytime.

McKenzie remembers the last miner who packed up his belongings and left Livingstone, in 1945. He was Alf Adams, who also ran the local Post Office – presumably not an arduous task in this tiny town. If Adams had a distin-guishing mark in the goldfield community, it was for being a strict teetotaller.

McKenzie attended primary school at Livingstone with about seven other pupils in the 1940s. He heard of an early teacher who was in charge of the schools at Livingstone and Island Cliff, a few kilometres apart, at the same time. The busy man taught at one school in the morning, then rode his horse to the other for the afternoon. The school at Island Cliff closed in 1937. Livingstone School lived on until 1963.

Livingstone today is a clutch of old build-ings where abandoned cars and horse-drawn contraptions die slowly from rust and rot in the shade of trees that were already ancient when Depression diggers straggled up here seeking work.

On a low hill is the cemetery. I remark on how few graves it seems to contain. McKenzie points out that about 120 miners and labourers were buried here in unmarked graves. Perhaps they were paupers, loners, men on the run. Little or nothing was known of them. Over time, their graves became overgrown and their section of the cemetery was deemed an eye-sore. So the ground was levelled and has been kept mown since.

As mentioned in a previous chapter, Gabriel Read discovered gold at the Tuapeka, thereby starting the Otago gold rushes in 1861. Not as widely known is the fact that an Indian, known at the time as Black Peter, had found gold in the Tuapeka area significantly earlier than Read. Perhaps because he was Indian, no one took much notice of him. But Read did. The rest is history, as they say.

Also not well known is that Read had prospected widely in Otago and Southland before reaching the Tuapeka. And he continued prospecting after. Only days after his historic find he made another discovery, at Waitahuna Valley, some 15 kilometres east of Gabriels Gully.

A rush followed and twin towns rose up at Waitahuna Valley and Waitahuna. The names must have been confusing for mail deliverers. The former died out but the latter is hanging on, just. The school is still open but businesses have closed. Waitahuna's position on State Highway 8 to Central Otago and the former Roxburgh railway branch line boosted its growth at the expense of Waitahuna Valley, which had been the larger town.

Two women who were brought up in the Waitahuna area in the 1940s escort me up the valley in 2014. They ask not to be named so I call them Pinot and Riesling, as wine is supposed to improve with age.

A few kilometres up the valley stands a memorial to the prospectors who found gold here in 1861. It was erected in 1948, against the backdrop of a steep rock face. Pinot and Riesling remember the unveiling ceremony well.

A few miners continued working here through the 1940s. Pinot and Riesling remember the last ones riding their bikes to their claims, with shovels tied to the bars of the bikes. They recall visits here by the gold buyer from a Lawrence bank. He did business with one digger at a time in a small tin shed while a queue waited outside with small bags of gold to sell.

Little trace remains of Waitahuna Valley township. Look carefully, though, and you can discern where narrow lanes ran a short distance up one side of the valley. Simple cottages once lined these lanes. Among the residents was a community of several Norwegian families. Their menfolk were diggers, but not of gold. They came to dig water races for sluicing the gold.

Among the stories Pinot and Reisling tell is a reminiscence of the last Chinese digger in the area. He walked the six kilometres into Waitahuna each week for groceries. On that day he changed from the work clothes that he had stitched from sugar bags, into his only suit. He walked most of the way on bare feet with his only pair of shoes tied together and slung around his neck. Nearing the town, he put the shoes on and when he headed back, he took them off again.

Opposite left: The scale of work at New Zealand's largest operating gold mine is something usually associated with Australian mining scenes. Old diggings at Macraes Flat, inland from Palmerston, were re-opened by OceanaGold in 1990.

Opposite right: Gold diggings in North Otago? Livingstone, I presume. John McKenzie remembers the last miners who worked the Livingstone goldfield – jobless men who had come during the Depression and stayed on after. Some lived in cob huts like this one. McKenzie enjoys sharing the local history with visitors to the hills behind Duntroon, in the Waitaki Valley.

Going back down the valley we pass a crumbling stone cottage. Pinot says an Italian family lived there. This goldfield really was an international concern.

What would happen when the gold ran out must have been a concern too. Pinot says miners had to register to dig for gold. Their registration allowed them to "squat" (live free of rent) on sections of land big enough for a family to sustain itself. The land they occupied remained in public ownership and was known as "commonage".

Waitahuna's commonage remains to this day. An elected trust board administers it and leases most of it to neighbouring farmers for grazing. The revenue from the leases is paid as grants to worthy causes in the Waitahuna-Lawrence district.

Waitahuna Valley was big enough at its peak to warrant the building in 1905 of a grand suspension bridge across the Waitahuna River. It still stands as a silent memorial but is seldom seen as busy travellers rush across the river on the State Highway 8 bridge at Waitahuna, several kilometres downstream.

The valley town supported a typical array of shops, a Post Office, hotels, a hall, a mining warden, a police camp with court house and jail, and that trademark of Otago gold towns, an athenaeum. This was a centre of adult learning, a library-come-lecture hall-come lounge where men could sit and smoke and discuss matters philosophical (and otherwise).

Forty minutes upcountry on State Highway 8 brings you to Millers Flat. This busy little place is one of the more enduring gold towns.

Above: This suspension bridge is a relic of the Otago gold rushes. It spans Waitahuna Creek, near the abandoned Waitahuna Valley township. A short distance downstream is the township of Waitahuna, its existence assured by the now-defunct Roxburgh branch railway and the highway "Up Central".

The handsome 1899 Clutha River bridge that leads into the town seems to span history as well as water.

I arrive here in 2012 wondering if I will find a knowledgeable resident to tell me about the place. A trick that always works is to ask the school secretary for suggestions. I do this and she, helpful in the way of all school secretaries, refers me to Betty Adams who compiled the area's history for the school's centenary in 1986 and is now updating it.

Millers Flat was the offspring of the many gold dredges that operated along the stretch of Clutha River between Ettrick and Beaumont, Adams says. Dredge workers and their families, and the usual range of merchants and mechanics, plus the scattered few runholders, their workers and families, kept the town going.

The dredges were a mixed blessing. The spoil they left in long piles behind them altered the river's course, bringing flood waters into the town. Strong currents damaged the ramps on the river's banks where the punt operated to carry people and goods across the river. This led to the building of the bridge, which is still in use.

As gold recovery declined, one by one the dredges were dismantled and the parts removed. Adams says some of the men who had worked on the dredges chose to stay. They bought small blocks of land beside the river that were offered cheaply. Taking advantage of strong Central Otago sunshine, shelter from the hills to the south, and water

Left: The importance of railways in rural areas is shown in the location of Millers Flat. The township was situated beside the Roxburgh branch railway line. The highway to Central Otago was stranded on the far bank, accessible only by ferry, until this bridge was built. The bridge still serves but the railway is long gone.

pumped from the river, they developed apricot and cherry orchards. Thus they were among pioneers of the region's famous stone fruit industry.

As these settlers prospered, some took advantage of the government's policy of "breaking up" large estates around the country. They bought blocks of pastoral land and moved into sheep farming.

Further again "up Central" the remains of gold diggings recline in the custodial arms of romance and legend. When I first visited Bannockburn and Bendigo in the 1970s it was as if the diggers had just trudged off and left their world for curious latecomers to stumble upon a century later.

I return to Bannockburn on a Heartland trip in 2006 to find some changes. Grape vines now line the gentler slopes. Generations of harrier hawks that once scanned the earth from their gliding undulations, seeking rabbit carrion, have gone. I guess myxamatosis has removed rabbit from the menu. The old blokes in the pub who trotted out reminiscences of scratching through the deserted diggings in the Depression for traces of gold have all passed away.

But here to stay, I hope, are the indelible marks of gold mining: shambling remnants of stone huts; bits of rusted iron from ancient mechanical devices; fractured hillsides bared and bleached by the sun; half-slumped channels that brought water from high in the back country for the sluice guns; shafts and tunnel entrances where you must take care not to stumble.

The most striking relic is a vast man-made pond at a place called Stewart Town. Dozens of workers must have slaved here to pile stone upon stone and create a wall that would hold water in this rectangular reservoir. How big? I estimate about the size of three football fields.

Stewart Town was one of a series of settlements for the miners and Bannockburn was their main centre. It was bigger then, a worthy rival to Cromwell, across the Kawarau River.

Modern Cromwell has rebuilt parts of its heritage as a museum of the golden days. Bannockburn is a museum of the golden days – if you ignore the grapes.

On the Carrick Range above Bannockburn I see remains of water-wheels and stamping batteries, used to crush quartz rock so the gold within could be recovered. They dot the highland. They are ages old, though they could pass as modern art installations.

Further inland, at Arrowtown, is the finest goldfields museum I have seen. When I visit in 2008 I find Arrowtown has become a tourist destination. It has even redeveloped the old Chinatown. If that were not enough, it cashes in on a riotous past that endears it to visitors with a keen sense of imagination – a mix of fact and fiction about a boom town where booze, fist fights, girlie shows, gambling and prostitution ruled.

Village Association chairman Richard Newman enthuses about the "feeling of history" that is palpable down the original main street with its authentic heritage buildings.

"There is a lesson to other towns – look after your history," Newman says.

I am not sure that well-curated history, as at Arrowtown and Cromwell, is any more evocative than the neglected and fading memorabilia of the golden age, as at Bannockburn and Bendigo. But then, I am not an Australian or Chinese visitor cramming as many sights onto a camera card as a package tour deal can allow.

Opposite: "Stately in Stewart Town," the land agents might say. This substantial stone cottage reflects the wealth achieved by miners at Stewart Town, on the Bannockburn diggings, south of Cromwell. Or perhaps the owner was the boss of a large sluicing operation and left the "hard yacka" to others. Nearby are the remains of a stone reservoir built by hand for the sluicing.

Below: Timber was scarce in Central Otago as few trees flourished in the extremes of the region's climate. But schist was abundant, so the pioneers built in stone. The hills of Bendigo, north of Cromwell, are partly covered in grape vines now but remnants of mining settlements remain scattered across the former goldfield.

CHAPTER 7

Forging links

GETTING AROUND AND RELAYING information could be difficult in this small country of scattered settlements divided by rivers and ranges. The growth of modes of communication was vital to developing a "one nation" ethos.

Stories about the establishment of communications systems have produced some interesting characters. One such man of recent times is Peter Dickson.

The boatman, ferry master and skipper has sole command of a vessel that is unique in the Southern Hemisphere. He drives a punt across the mighty Clutha River. It is the last remaining punt of some 50 that once carried horses, carts, people, goods, and later cars, over the river from gold rush times.

The punt, a flat-bottomed barge, blunt at each end and sitting on two pontoons, looks like a floating bridge. It is old. So is Dickson. It is powered solely by river currents, harnessed by wire ropes and pulleys.

I am about to leave Gore and head for home in 2007 after gathering information in Southland for Heartland columns in *The Press*. The drive to Christchurch takes about seven hours so I have time for a short detour to Tuapeka Mouth to see if the punt is still operating there.

While living in Lawrence in the early 1970s, I saw the punt on the Clutha at Tuapeka Mouth. A township existed at "the Mouth" then. People used the punt as it provided a river crossing on the most direct link between Lawrence and Gore.

In 2007 I take one of the several roads that leave State Highway 1 and drift through picturesque farmland to the township of Clydevale, on the Clutha River. What a fitting combination of names that is, as Clutha is Gaelic for Clyde.

I cross the bridge at Clydevale and turn upstream for the 10 kilometres beside the Clutha to Tuapeka Mouth. With the bridge at Clydevale so close, surely the punt is no longer in use, I wonder. But it is worth checking.

Tuapeka Mouth grew up as a farm-service township just below the point where the Tuapeka River pours into the Clutha. It is almost a ghost town now. Houses, shops, garage, church, school _ all seem abandoned and unkempt. The weatherboard buildings have been turned a pale gray by the South Otago climate. Flickering shadows from tree branches waving in the breeze add a spooky element.

Dickson has lived all his life here. He may be the sole resident. He remembers Tuapeka Mouth as a thriving settlement before World War II.

Opposite: A tour bus toils up the road from Milford Sound to the Homer Tunnel. The road is a credit to workers who pushed through almost impregnable terrain to link such remote places. Credit also to Christchurch man Ernie Collins who became the first non-employee on the project to walk through the tunnel.

Down by the river, though, life goes on. A ramp dips down to the punt, tied securely to a hitching post. Halfway down the ramp stands a structure that resembles a sentry box outside Buckingham Palace. A car's side mirror has been fastened to the door so the "sentry" can see any car approaching down the ramp.

Dickson sees me. Out he comes, slipping his captain's peaked cap on his head, and stumps up to me. His old black labrador waddles along behind.

He is delighted to be interviewed. He tells me anecdotes of his many years in this job. One is about a woman who drove her automatic car gingerly onto the punt and then, in a sense of panic, hit the accelerator instead of the brake. The car thrust forward and plunged into the swirling waters.

The car was fairly watertight, says Dickson. It floated a few metres before "bellying" on a submerged rock. And there it sat while he summoned emergency services and the poor woman was rescued.

He tells of floods, such as the one that overflowed the bank and the ramp and left its watermark more than halfway up the wall of his "sentry box". He shows me the line he carved in the wall as a permanent sign of the water level.

Had it not been for a massive clump of flax bushes stopping it, the "sentry box" would certainly have been washed away, he says.

Dickson remembers old-timers years ago telling him of the steamboats

that once chugged upriver from Balclutha, past Tuapeka Mouth, almost to Beaumont. Farmers, runholders and storekeepers built landings beside the river where passengers and freight were loaded and unloaded.

I tell Dickson I am surprised the punt still operates, especially as the bridge at Clydevale is only a few minutes away.

"Ah well," he replies in a resigned tone, "We are only open at peak traffic times now."

"Er, and what are peak traffic times here?" I ask.

"Eight to ten in the morning and three to five in the afternoon," he says crisply.

I look at my watch. It is 9.15am. I look up the ramp to the road above. I gaze across the river to the far ramp. Not another vehicle or person is in sight.

He asks me if I want to take a ride on the punt. It is free, as the local council funds it from the tourism budget. But we have talked too long for me to take a return crossing and get home in good time. So I promise to come back another day.

This promise is kept in 2012 and Dickson takes me across in my car. It is uncanny watching the 79-year-old manipulate the wire ropes so the craft, entirely without motive power, veers left and right as it runs across the strong currents of the Clutha. It berths at exactly the right point of the ramp on the opposite bank, about six minutes after starting. A camper van is waiting there to cross back, so I thank Dickson and drive away.

Above right: A natural sand causeway sweeps across Cable Bay to Pepin Island, near Nelson. Into this bay came New Zealand's first international communications cable. The cable provided a direct link with Sydney, which joined New Zealand to an international cable network. No longer did New Zealanders have to wait weeks for news from Britain and Europe.

A boatie later explains the punt's progress across the river movements as similar to the zig-zag course of a yacht tacking across the wind.

How much did communications depend on river punts in colonial times? And how do they compare with the power of cables to carry telegraphic messages across the world?

A road sign near Nelson points towards Cable Bay. One day, I will go there, I often said to myself as I passed the corner. And one day, in 2013, I do.

A recent storm has caused soil and clay to slip off the soggy hills and onto the road. Traffic is held up while work gangs are clearing the slips. So the five-minute drive blows out to 12. But it is worth it to reach the bay and, across it to the right, see beautiful Pepin Island.

At a camping ground in the village I meet Tony Smith, a refugee from the frantic world of big business who has chosen to live out his days in idyllic ease and a luxury caravan.

Smith introduces me to Barbara Stuart. She and husband Ian own and run the camp and a farm on the hills behind it. Ian's grandparents bought Pepin Island 90 years ago and farmed it before buying land here and moving across the natural causeway.

The question that has been burning in me is, why is this place called Cable Bay? The answer is simple _ yet astonishing. This little-known and fairly isolated spot was the landing place of the first international communications cable in New Zealand. The under-sea cable from Sydney came ashore here in 1876. This was about 15 years after cables were first used within New Zealand, to carry reports from ships arriving at ports to eager readers in the main towns around the country.

The international cable connected New Zealand to the world, via Australia, nearly half a century after the first white settlers had arrived. Now reports of events in Europe and America could reach New Zealand within a few hours, instead of the weeks it had taken by sailing ship.

A village grew up here for the 30 staff at the cable station and their families. I ask Barbara where the cable station stood and she shows me some concrete foundations that are all that is left of it. Next to the site is a tennis court that the Stuarts have almost finished restoring for their campers to use. It is on a patch of flat ground where the cable station staff had built the first tennis court, though that had fallen into disrepair.

The station burned down in 1914, Barbara says. The cable still worked but the whole operation was transferred to Titahi Bay, near Wellington, three years later.

Cable Bay today is home to a dozen-or-so families who commute daily to Nelson for work and school. Another dozen-or-so houses fill up at weekends and holidays as "getaways".

They come to Cable Bay for kayaking, snorkelling, swimming and fishing, or just to feast on the birdsong and scenery. Some drive, others take the active approach, on the Cable Bay Walkway.

The Stuarts tell me of a time when the peace of the bay was shattered. The sailing ship Delaware was driven by a storm onto rocks off Pepin Island. The small Maori community there rallied under the leadership of Huria Matenga to rescue the passengers and crew. She organised the rescuers into a human chain. Working in high winds and stinging spray they got nearly everyone off the stricken ship and safely to shore. One man perished. He was a crewman who became trapped in a hold while searching for anyone left behind.

Matenga then led the castaways to the pa where hot food was prepared for them and blankets were wrapped around them.

This happened in 1863, when wars in the North Island were straining Maori-Pakeha relations. It would have been a front-page story for all the newspapers. But no cable existed at Cable Bay then to convey the news. People through most of New Zealand would not have known of it for days.

If shipping was the key to New Zealand's early links with the world, then Port Chalmers was the door. The deepwater port nestles in a bay halfway along the north-eastern side of Otago Harbour, 12 minutes drive from downtown Dunedin.

The pride of New Zealand shipping for many years was the Union Steamship Company. This line was born in Port Chalmers and became the largest in the Southern Hemisphere as its vessels circumnavigated the world.

Port Chalmers has a history to be proud of and a band of men who take pride in preserving it. I find the "old salts" already hard at work early on a winter's morning in 2014. As volunteer labourers, with maritime backgrounds, they are helping to build an extension to the town's museum. The impressive addition, to be called The Boat Shed, will house shipping exhibits.

They point out the nearby spot where local Maori leaders negotiated and signed the deed of sale for the Otago Land Block to the New Zealand Land Company. The Maori called this place Koputai. The name referred to an incident in which an unusually high tide washed away a large canoe that had been drawn up on the beach. So, even in pre-European times, this was a shipping port.

This seemed the best place for immigrant settler ships to dock and a village grew up here in the 1840s. The first ships bringing Scottish settlers as part of the planned colonisation of the Otago (Otakau) area sailed into Port Chalmers in 1848.

A hotel already stood near the wharves. Though substantially re-built, it still stands and stakes its claim as the oldest hotel in continuous operation south of Nelson.

"Old salt" Harold Woods says Port Chalmers made its name nationally as a centre for boat building and ship repairs. Two dry docks opened in 1872. He trained as a diver and sheetmetal worker in the 1950s. He later specialised in underwater welding to repair metal hull plates on vessels that needed a quick turnaround and could not afford time in dry dock.

Port Chalmers was home to many marine engineering firms, and ship building continued down the ages, Woods says. The yard built seven minesweepers for the navy in World War II. They served in the Pacific Islands. Several fishing trawlers were built here. Major repair work was done on American ships visiting the Antarctic and on a Russian deep-sea trawler.

Below: A new addition to the Port Chalmers Museum has been named The Boat Shed. Its exhibits give some idea of the old port's historic significance and the many national "firsts" that were achieved there. The expanded and modernised port remains one of the country's busiest.

A notable milestone in Port Chalmers' history was the departure of New Zealand's first export consignment of frozen meat on the refrigerated ship Dunedin, for England, in 1882. Otago's port was a pioneer again, 90 years later, when the ship Columbus departed for the USA with New Zealand's first containerised export cargo.

The town of Port Chalmers seems to have changed only little in about 100 years. Stately old buildings from the Victorian and Edwardian eras still front the hillside and the friendly streets where locals all know one another.

But the port would be unrecognisable to old-timers returning after a long time away. Lumbering truck and trailer units haul whole forests of pine logs through the electronic gates. On newly reclaimed land gigantic cranes like aliens from The War of the Worlds scoff metal containers and spit them out on ships as long as rugby fields. Mobile cranes zip in and out of a suburb of containers stacked densely and as high as a city apartment block.

Port Chalmers brings the world to Otago, and Otago to the world.

At the other end of the scale is the forgotten little port of Saltwater Creek, in North Canterbury. Long ago this was known as Northport. Here small coastal vessels of the so-called "mosquito fleet" loaded wool bales from the pastoral runs of the Amuri, Hurunui and Kowai areas. Like little shunting railway locomotives, the vessels delivered supplies to, and collected export cargo from ports along the Canterbury coast and as far north as southern Marlborough. Loads of wool were marshalled at Lyttelton for transfer to the ocean-going ships that would carry them to England.

A few decaying wharf piles poking above the languid surface of Saltwater Creek are reminders of this link in New Zealand's communications chain. The wooden piles have lasted well. For, the mosquito fleet was largely redundant by the end of the 1800s. Their era ended once the wide Canterbury rivers were bridged and bullocks or horses could haul wool wagons to the nearest railway yards.

I explore Saltwater Creek one day in 2012. It is truly a creek in the British understanding of the word _ that is, an inlet, _ rather than the Kiwi idea of a smallish river. The incoming tide at Pegasus Bay pushes sea water up the Ashley River lagoon and its near-neighbour, the Saltwater Creek, near Waikuku Beach.

Most times when I cross the bridge on State Highway 1 the water seems to be motionless. Rather than flow, it just swells and recedes with the cycle of the tides. The sea is only a kilometre away but Saltwater Creek meanders in a great loop through low-lying ground, stretching the distance to about two kilometres. Boats would cover this distance upstream on the rising tide, and tie up at the wharf.

Where today you might see some whitebaiters studying the water in seemingly somnolent pose, or families enjoying a picnic at the tables on the reserve area, once the garrulous calls and commands of boat crew must have rent the air.

Where now you have to raise your voice to be heard against the roar of huge trucks crossing the bridge, you once would have been lulled by the rhythmic clomp of Clydesdale hooves as Leithfield carrier James Ashworth guided another of his wagons to unload wool at the wharf.

As late as the 1960s, a store and a garage still operated above the north bank of Saltwater Creek. But the school, which opened a century earlier, with space for 90 pupils, had long closed. The Post Office and a pub that stood a little further up the road, stand only in history now. Old bridge abutments show where the road used to twist and turn to cross the river where the banks were highest.

The mosquito fleet served other river ports too, most notably Kaiapoi. In areas where there was no suitable river, the boats had to wait offshore while wool was transferred from wagons standing in the surf to lighters that were then rowed to the boats and re-loaded into their holds.

Ward Beach, by the mouth of the Flaxbourne River, south of Blenheim, was one place where this potentially treacherous operation was carried out.

Flaxbourne was one of the earliest and greatest of the South Island sheep stations, founded by one of New Zealand's first Premiers (Prime Ministers), Frederick Weld, and Charles Clifford.

Below: Highway traffic on the Saltwater Creek bridge, north of Christchurch, pays no heed to an old wharf pile. Once known as Northport, Saltwater Creek rang to the cries of teamsters and sailors as wool was transferred from wagons to boats that had sailed up the winding tidal creek. Signs remain of a township that surrounded this industrious scene.

As the expected arrival times of boats could never be specific, wool bales were stockpiled in a large shed where the township of Ward now stands, about one kilometre east of State Highway 1. The shed is still standing and I take a look through it in 2013. It is clear from the photos on the wall how difficult it must have been to row the lighter past jagged rocks where spume sprayed wildly and through the breaking waves to the waiting boat. Then the big, weighty bales had to be hoisted from the little craft as it rolled in the sea swell, up to the deck of the coastal vessel as it swayed too.

The shape of the South Island made early communication between east and west coasts difficult. So tricky could it be to traverse the Southern Alps that some gold diggers bound from Christchurch to Hokitika preferred the sea passage. Much of Canterbury's expected economic windfall from West Coast gold discoveries never eventuated, as crossing the Tasman Sea to Melbourne or Sydney seemed easier than making contact with Christchurch.

So the order went out: "Find a viable pass through the mountains".

Groups of Maori had been using mountain passes for generations, of course. But they did not have to consider horses and they had slaves to carry their heavy loads of pounamu.

In another chapter we look at Arthur Dudley Dobson finding the pass that came to bear his first name. A road and a railway line were pushed through it. The road is now a state highway. Similarly, roads through the Lewis and Haast passes have become highways.

Below: Inside the red shed at Ward, south of Blenheim, are relics of a bygone age. When Flaxbourne Station was a major pastoral run, produce was stored in the shed until a coastal vessel arrived off Ward Beach. It was then taken by surf boat to be loaded into the ship at anchor. The red shed sits a kilometre east of State Highway 1.

No matter how many times I drive the Haast Pass it still surprises me how easy its gradients are. It is the lowest of the three main passes, with its summit a mere 564 metres above sea level.

In 2005 I find the road sealed all the way, though a "runaway vehicle ramp" as a refuge for speedsters at one tricky bend is a reminder that this is perilous terrain. Later, in Haast, I meet Don Rose. He is a bit grumpy about the sealing of the road. It is bringing too many tourists into the region, he complains.

He came here in 1979 to get away from the rat race. Now the rat race has come to join him. Hundreds of tourists fill all the hotel and motel beds in the area each night, he says.

Rose worked in helicopter deer recovery but says that industry has tailed off, as have fishing and sawmilling, while farming is at a low ebb. So, begrudgingly he admits tourism is a necessary evil.

In rugged parts of the pass I have to wonder how a road was ever constructed here. The answer lies in the large areas of flat land south of Haast township. You can see signs of a public works camp that stood here in the road-building days. The road through here, from as far south as Jackson Bay, appears to have been sealed many years ago. This allowed heavy machinery and massive road engineering items, that were shipped to Jackson Bay for unloading at the wharf, to be easily transported by road up into the pass.

Lewis Pass does not share the excess of tourists that bugs Don Rose at Haast. The Lewis is the highest pass of the big three and its main problem is excessive snow.

So says Akira Matsushita, part-owner and manager, with Takako Ogino, of the Maruia Springs thermal resort. The Japanese couple bought the resort in 1991. It comprises a tourist hotel and hot mineral spa bathing areas, beside the Maruia River at the bottom of the long hill that plunges, westward, from the summit of the pass.

When I visit them in 2008 they are still talking about a recent big snowfall. Matsushita says he usually welcomes snow as it gives the resort a romantic appearance that enthrals visitors. Guests love it because they can soak in hot outdoor pools and savour the snow-coated scene, without having to swat sandflies, he says.

But the 2008 snowfall was different. It tested the resort's systems, facilities and staff as they had never been tested before. Matsushita has never seen such a snowfall. The sheer weight of it toppled trees that blocked roads, crushed water pipelines and broke the pump that drew hot water from the spring. Poles, lines, aerials and the electricity generator failed. Only satellite computer connection, which relied on batteries, kept the resort in touch with the outside world.

The decision to close the resort had to be made. Guests had to pack up and leave. Many were reluctant to go but they got out just in time, Matsushita says. Minutes later, the Lewis Pass road was closed to all traffic.

The staff stayed, but for two weeks Maruia Springs was cut off. Matsushita, an experienced helicopter pilot, managed to fly in equipment from Christchurch to fix and replace damaged infrastructure. The mainly Japanese staff, with little idea of such work, "got stuck in" to help with repairs. When the road opened again, the resort was ready to greet a new wave of tourists and travellers.

Kiwi ingenuity? The Japanese have it too.

Some might argue the road from Te Anau to Milford Sound is a pass through the Southern Alps. True or not, it is, to my mind, New Zealand's premier tourist drive. The mountain views from your bus windows as you approach the Homer Tunnel are unequalled in this country – and many others.

The opening of the 1270 metres-long tunnel was both an engineering feat and a huge leap forward in development of the tourist industry. I have driven, and been driven, through the tunnel nearly a dozen times and marvelled at it each time. In 2009 I interview a man who went through it illegally, while it was still under construction.

Such was the excitement being generated by the tunnel building project that Ernie Collins, then 19, set off from his Christchurch home in 1941. His aim was to be the first person not attached to a work crew to pass through the tunnel. As late as 2009 he has still never heard of anyone who might have beaten him to that distinction.

Collins put his bike on the train at Christchurch and travelled in comfort on the Invercargill Express as far as Gore. He then took a train on the Waimea branch line to Lumsden. From there he cycled the mainly shingle road to Te Anau. He had packed his bike with camping gear and tells me he was "just about dead" when he reached the lakeside town at 9pm.

Next day he rode as far as Cascade Creek, on the Milford Road. The following day he reached the Homer Tunnel portal, after walking his bike on the last uphill grade.

Here he met a different sort of challenge. Some workmen took an interest in him. They led him to the mess room for a meal and showed him a vacant hut where he could sleep. They told him he would have to get permission from their boss to go through the tunnel. Collins found the boss and put his request to him. Permission was declined.

His new mates were disappointed by their boss's refusal. Keen to see Collins succeed, they advised him to hide his bike in the hut and then sneak into the tunnel when the day shift of workers knocked off and before the night shift took over.

It would be pitch black inside, so he should take a torch, they said. The plan worked and Collins passed through the steeply declining tunnel where water gushed from cracks in the walls and roof to form puddles and saturate the clay on the rough and rock-strewn floor.

As he reached the western end, some workers called out to him but he took no notice and kept on walking until he was in open air again.

The road from the tunnel down to Milford Sound had not been completed yet, Collins says, so he had to negotiate a rough track through native bush by moonlight.

Reaching the Cleddau Valley, he found a road leading to Milford Sound. There was a vacant hut there so he slept the rest of the night in it before proceeding. Next morning he followed the road to the little fishing and tourist village at the sound. There was nothing to do there so, with a faint feeling of anti-climax, he turned around and began the climb back to the tunnel.

Collins says he had no plan for getting through the tunnel again but he had achieved what he had set out to do and was not too worried about it. Lucky for him, a works truck pulled up beside him. The man in the passenger seat asked what Collins was doing. He seemed impressed by Collins' answer and offered him a lift. Taking passengers was forbidden, the man said, so Collins had to jump up on the deck and lie low. If he was caught, he must say the men up front did not know he was there.

When they reached the end of the road at the Cleddau, Collins jumped down from the truck, wondering what to do next. The decision was made for him when the man in the passenger seat took him aside.

The man told Collins he was a surveyor. He said to Collins: "You are my chain man. Stick with me and speak to no one".

Then, carrying items of surveying equipment between them, the pair walked the bush track up to the tunnel, entered it and, half-an-hour later, emerged at the eastern portal.

The workers who had helped Collins on his way were thrilled at his achievement and celebrated with drinks in their huts that night. Collins then took a day's rest before mounting his bike again and starting the long journey home.

He remembers a downpour of rain that left him soaked and being taken in by some roadmen at a camp in the Eglinton Valley, where a roaring fire dried him and a hot meal revived him.

It was Collins' last great adventure before enlisting for service with the Fleet Air Arm in World War II.

The gold town of Lyell almost died from lack of communications. Its redemption came from a most unexpected source, a man who had left his Greek Island home as a boy, had gone to sea and jumped ship in New Zealand to escape a cruel skipper.

Taken in by an Irish couple, whose daughter he later married, he took up the job of running river boats up the Buller River from Westport.

He was Nicholas Demetriou Mangos, revered by all at Lyell in the 1860s and 1870s. He was known to them as Peter the Greek.

Lyell was a rich goldfield and one of the earliest in the Buller region. The town perched on a steep hillside above the north bank of the Buller River, in the gorge between Murchison and Inangahua Junction.

Below: For the families of gold mining town Lyell, in the Upper Buller Gorge, communication with the world was by boat on the Buller River. The substantial town faced famine when the boats could not get through. No wonder everyone left when the gold ran out. Only a few graves remain.

Almost nothing today remains of the town. The land where it stood has been cleared and is a popular camping and picnic spot. Historic photographs on billboards there show the scale of the town, where the fronts of tall buildings roost on piles up the main street.

For decades Lyell was cut off from the rest of civilization. No road pierced the dense bush on these near-vertical hills. No telegraph wires reached here. Access was by river only.

But the Buller River was no friend to the traveller. Many a boat was lost, with its cargo, on the river journey of several days. Frequent floods and swift flows moved massive boulders that altered the river's course, so underwater dangers could never be charted.

One man, though, always managed to get through. Mangos never failed to deliver his freight and his passengers. And that was the saving of Lyell, where soil and climate made gardening and cropping impossible, where stock would not thrive and, given a sniff of freedom, would get lost in the bush.

When floods prevented river boats from reaching Lyell, and before difficult mountain tracks were improved to allow pack horses to get through, the people of the town faced starvation from time to time. Mangos was indeed their saviour.

Visiting in 2011, I read information on Lyell from the interpretative boards there. I see a wooden cross and stone cairn commemorating a Norman Patrick Mangos, who died in 2006, aged 80. Clearly too young to be Peter the Greek, he was surely one of the old boatman's descendants.

A more modern example of communications can be seen only from the outside, near the central Marlborough town of Renwick.

Two XOS golf balls, each taller than a two-storeyed house, stand in a paddock up the Waihopai Valley. Their prominence is enhanced by the contrast of their Persil whiteness against the backdrop of the drought-charred Wither Hills.

But this is no golf course. Signs along the roadside indicate something sneaky about this place. The warnings are terse: dare to trespass here and you will be dragged before the commanding officer of Royal NZ Air Force Base Woodbourne, which is back down the road.

Reading the notices in 2011, my mind goes into overdrive producing visions of some apoplectic Biggles character with quivering moustache ordering me to be flung into the cooler for the maximum 90 days.

The reality of Waihopai is not funny, though. Even if an attack on these "golf balls" in 2008 sparked a saga that many news followers found amusing.

I note a clue to what may be going on at Waihopai in the name of a nearby winery _ "Spy Valley". A receptionist here tells me the winery's name "was inspired by the spy station". She adds that the winery's

Opposite: Giant puffballs in a paddock at Waihopai, near Blenheim are highly sensitive, technically and politically. Peace protesters claim they link New Zealand to the United State's world-wide spying network. In a celebrated sabotage case, three upper-middle-aged men foiled base security and damaged the domes with sickels. They were acquitted.

newsletter, which is sent to regular customers, is called "The Spy Ring".

This is all in good fun, of course. The winery representative assures me the people at the "spy station" have always been great neighbours.

Nevertheless, allegations are often heard of electronic spying on New Zealand citizens carried out at Waihopai as part of a world-wide surveillance network providing intelligence to super-power USA.

Such allegations led three activists to vandalise the "golf balls" in 2008. The three entered this forbidden territory, armed with sickles. Once inside, they slashed the protective covering of one of the spherical objects before security staff apprehended them.

In a matter of minutes, three old men with sickles got through the gate, crossed 300-metres of open paddock to the first "golf ball", hacked away at its cover and did damage that would cost $1 million dollars to prepare.

Those three men, all peace activists and one a Catholic priest, somehow escaped the wrath of the senior air force officer at Woodbourne. However, they were charged in a civil court with unlawful entry and intentional damage. They pleaded guilty as charged but in mitigation claimed their actions had been intended to save victims of war and torture. They believed the Waihopai base was aiding the American-led invasion of Iraq as part of a war that, they claimed, was an offence against international law. It must have sounded convincing, as the judge discharged them.

The Waihopai "spy base" continues to operate, though you have to think its security blokes should have been told to smarten up their act. Perhaps they should have been flung into the cooler for 90 days.

Whatever else this case shows, it certainly indicates how far communications have come in New Zealand, from the days of plodding pack horses and lighters loading wool bales in the surf, to satellites observing strange events in our heartland and relaying evidence to The Pentagon in Washington.

CHAPTER 8

The Midas touch

HERE'S A GOOD QUIZ QUESTION: what object in New Zealand history was known as the Honourable Roddy?

Answer: the largest gold nugget ever found on a New Zealand goldfield.

How big? Well, at 3.6 kilograms it was about as heavy as seven packs of butter, though in size only about as big as one. In today's dollar values it would be worth hundreds of thousands.

The nugget was found at Ross, New Zealand's richest alluvial goldfield, in 1909. It was named after the Minister of Mines at that time, the Honourable Roderick McKenzie. The nugget was sold for £400 and raffled as a fundraiser for a new hospital. The government then bought it and presented it to King George V as a gesture of loyalty. Sadly, it was later melted down and used to gild cutlery at Buckingham Palace. Oh well.

Ross is about 20 minutes south of Hokitika. Discovery of gold there and around Hokitika in 1864 launched the West Coast gold rush. Diggers poured in, even from the still-active goldfields of Central Otago. If they sought warmer winters, they would have got them. They would also have got a lot wetter.

The West Coast breeds characters. One of them is Evan Birchfield. I meet him at Ross in 2007 and we chat about his modern-day gold mining there. He tells me about his giant machinery unearthing deserted shafts and tunnels from the mining of more than a century ago.

When Birchfield restarted mining on the eastern side of Ross in 1990, his biggest problem was losing trucks. Heavily-laden trucks caused old shafts to collapse and several disappeared down them, he says. He had to bring bulldozers to the site and pull them out. Then came another problem. The truck drivers were not at all keen to get back behind the wheel.

Birchfield reckons he found so many tunnels, as far down as 45 metres, that whole rugby teams might have disappeared there from the nearby playing fields. This makes me wince, because I played a match there in 1967, totally unaware of any risk.

Work continued, though, and by 2003 Birchfield's excavation had turned a small hill into a massive hole. His next job was to restore the land and improve it.

The plan was to turn the opencast mine into a lake as the central feature of a recreational reserve. All went well until he tried to fill the lake with water. No matter how much water was allowed to pour in from the surrounding

Opposite: There's gold in them thar hills: This view of Cullensville looks south to the hills where gold was found and mined. Mt Cullen stands at the head of the valley that runs south from Linkwater, in the Marlborough Sounds area.
Marlborough Historical Society

hillsides, the lake level never rose. Birchfield sealed off some tunnels that he thought might have been draining the lake but still the lake kept losing water.

Birchfield says locals began joking about a Loch Ross Monster inhabiting the murky depths. They even arranged a fireworks display to lure the monster out.

Today that area of Ross is an attractive precinct of sports grounds and housing for the elderly. Standing above it is an informative museum where visitors can learn about the great days of Ross and the gold mining era that lasted 50 years until World War I. If they don't mind getting their hands wet, they can try panning for gold (under cover from the rain). Many thousands of tourists do.

Meanwhile, Birchfield has switched his attention to the west side of Ross. About two kilometres out of town, down towards the sea, his great lumbering machines continue to move the earth in the ongoing quest for gold.

The Honourable Roddy was a valuable nugget but it was greatly outweighed by another famous chunk of West Coast metal. This was the Londonderry Rock, near Kumara, north of Hokitika.

It is said that when the 3000-tonne rock toppled from the hillside where it had stood for thousands of years, the earth tremor it caused was so great it stopped the clock on the front of the Kumara Post Office, four kilometres away.

The area around Kumara was rich in gold. Mining was in full swing by the 1880s, including several sluicing and dredging operations. Some of the sluicing undermined the giant Londonderry Rock.

Gold was discovered at Greenstone, across the Taramakau River from here, in 1864. Local artist and environmentalist Carey Dillon tells me in 2007 this strike gave birth to the town of Kumara. Situated in the centre

Above: At Ross, south of Hokitika, gold mining still goes on. Evan Birchfield's company uses powerful modern machinery to extract gold that would have been inaccessible to the early diggers. There is another major difference, Birchfield says. Today's miners have to restore the land they dig up to pristine condition.

Below: Dating back to times when glaciers brought debris down from the mountains is Londonderry Rock. Estimated to weigh more than 3000 tonnes, the giant rock toppled with a gigantic thud when gold sluicing undermined it. Diggers could do nothing with it, so it still stands, undisturbed, a little east of the town of Kumara.

of a rich gold field, Kumara grew into a substantial town, with 47 hotels, five banks and a bush tramway providing a transport link with Greymouth. Around it were the diggings of Waimea (Goldsborough and Stafford), Dillmanstown and Greenstone.

Local historian Kerrie Fitzgibbon says the 1864 discovery of gold was made by two Maori searching for greenstone in the Hohonu Stream. Knowing how Maori treasured pounamu, I wonder if they were disappointed to have found gold instead.

Apparently not, as the pair tried to keep their find a secret, while they made the most of it. But word got out. Soon diggers were beating a path to the Hohonu Stream. The two Maori blocked the track through the bush to keep the diggers out. A confrontation followed. The situation blew up into a near riot, reflecting something of the Maori-Pakeha conflicts in the North Island at the time.

Reports of this row spread far and wide. Soon 300 mainly European miners were at work in Greenstone (as Hohonu was renamed).

Carey Dillon says local folklore tells of some young men discovering gold a short distance up the Taramakau Valley from Greenstone in the mid-1870s. As with the two Maori, the strike by these men was accidental too. They were digging and levelling a patch of land to erect an illicit whisky still, when they noticed traces of gold on their shovels.

Their efforts to keep their find secret failed too. One can only hope the rush of diggers that followed, and the establishment of Dillmanstown that ensued, proved productive for the whisky distilling plant.

As happened in most areas, Chinese miners followed. Fitzgibbon tells a sad tale of one of the last miners, a lone Chinese man who suffered from the dreaded leprosy. No one on the diggings would have anything to do with him for fear of the contagion. He became a prisoner in his own crude cabin. He was prohibited from entering Kumara, so a few kind souls left food for him at his gate. Eventually they found the parcels were no longer being collected. The poor man had died as he had lived – alone and far from home.

Visiting Greenstone in 2015, I can find only the cemetery to indicate where the settlement stood. Fitzgibbon tells me I am a decade too late to see the old jail house that stood across the road from there until it was pulled down.

Even the cemetery has had a makeover. I can see only four headstones, one of which has been relocated to stand in the gateway. All but one of the inscriptions have been rendered illegible by weathering. On the remaining one I can just decipher the words:

Left: Artist, conservationist and local historian Carey Dillon of Kumara values relics of the West Coast goldmining town's busy and prosperous past.

"Gerald McCormick … County Roscommon … 26 years … died 187-".

The cemetery's tidiness matches the well-ordered dairy farms up the lush Taramakau Valley. Milk is produced in great quantities here now. I doubt if whisky production ever got as big.

A plaque on an empty section in Kumara marks it as the former home of the town's most famous son, Richard John Seddon. Dubbed "King Dick", he was New Zealand's populist Premier (Prime Minister) from 1893 to 1906.

The Lancastrian arrived at the Waimea diggings, near Kumara, in 1866. He prospered as a digger and a miners' advocate and moved into Kumara 10 years later. There he established several businesses and became involved in politics.

Historical accounts of Seddon leave images of bluster and bellicosity. But when, in 2006, I climb the path to the Stafford Cemetery, tug the iron gate open and enter, I gain a different view of the big man. Among the graves, surrounded by tall trees, is one where two daughters of Seddon were buried. They died four years apart, in 1877 and 1881. Seddon was in his 30s then. As a father, I catch a vision of the tearful figure slumped by the graveside and my heart breaks for him.

The twin towns of Stafford and Goldsborough served the Waimea diggings at their peak in the 1870s. Together they were home to some 10,000 people. That was sufficient for a bush tramway to operate from Stafford to Hokitika. There is little evidence of all this today, though my attention is caught by a sign indicating where the Helvetia Hotel once stood. The name is indicative of some Swiss pioneers in the district.

Native trees stand among scrub on lower ground, while in the hills beyond exotic forest has replaced the bush. This is land that has been worked over for gold and then discarded as almost useless.

The diggers still come, though. I chat to some who return every year on their annual holidays. They come towing caravans to the camping ground and they fossick for any gold that the ghosts of these haunted spaces might have left behind.

Vic and Marie Chandler of Picton are typical 21st century prospectors. They pan in the streams by day and mix with other regulars over a few drinks in the evenings. They may find small traces of gold but they make large deposits of friendship.

Miners were hardy types. They toiled for gold as far south as Bruce Bay, halfway between Fox Glacier and Haast.

Bruce Bay resident John Birchfield (related to Evan Birchfield of Ross) loves introducing visitors to the history of the area. This is the place, he tells me in 2006, where legendary Maori hero Maui first set foot on Aotearoa. The local marae, rebuilt in 2005, is named Te Tauaka Waka a Maui, after the landing of Maui's canoe.

Birchfield also tells a great goldmining story. It is about Albert Hunt, a successful

Below: At Bruce Bay, John Birchfield walks in the footsteps of Maui. The legendary Maori hero landed at this South Westland spot 1000 years ago. The nearby marae is named Te Tauaka Waka a Maui – the landing place of Maui's canoe. The bay takes its name from a different craft – the paddle steamer Bruce that ferried prospectors up and down the West Coast until it was wrecked on the Grey River bar in 1867.

miner around Hokitika in the early gold rush days of the 1860s.

Hunt was getting sick of being followed by inept prospectors hoping he would lead them to a rich new field. So, in 1866, he bought a claim at Bruce Bay, fully aware there was no gold in the streams there. As soon as this became public knowledge 1000 hopeful prospectors tramped the long and difficult trail to Bruce Bay. A town of tents quickly sprang up and the diggers set to work.

Meanwhile, Hunt slipped away quietly and headed back to Hokitika. It must have been weeks before he heard the news from Bruce Bay – that the "duffers" (unsuccessful diggers) had been very brassed off at finding no gold and had raided and trashed the stores that merchants had set up at the bay.

Hunt might have smiled wryly but the last laugh was on him. For gold was found at Bruce Bay a little later, on the beach where access was easy and the digging was simpler. The mining settlement of Weldtown became established near where the tiny Bruce Bay village now stands.

The occasional fossicker still digs up the odd bit of gold on the beach, Birchfield says.

A working gold dredge on the Grey River at Ahaura is a more prominent sign of the continuing search for gold on the West Coast. Retired sawmiller John Beckwith has lived at Ahaura, north of Greymouth, since his mother bought the Ahaura Hotel in 1939. He was a teenager straight out of boarding school in Christchurch then.

Beckwith tells me in 2013 how he loved hearing the old-timers' stories of the gold days in his mother's pub through the 1940s.

A favourite character in old Ahaura was Benjamin Gough, an early hotelier. He could be seen as the archetypal goldminer, says Beckwith.

Born in Ireland, Gough went to sea as a boy, jumped ship to try his luck on the diggings in California, then switched to the Australian goldfields. He crossed the Tasman when he heard of Gabriel Read's strike at the Tuapeka in 1861. Moving further up Central Otago, Gough joined a group of miners who found a rich gold field at present-day Arrowtown and managed to keep it secret for some weeks.

Below: Who says the golden days are gone? On the West Coast, they may be here to stay. This gold dredge on the Grey River at Ahaura is one of several mining ventures still under way.

Gough settled at Ahaura in 1866. He used the wealth he had accumulated to buy a small farm and a hotel. He married, raised a family and became a leading citizen.

Further north again is the town of Reefton. And 10 kilometres up the road from there is Cronadun, its name yet another reminder that many gold miners were of Irish extraction.

Peter Walsh grew up at Cronadun in the 1950s. He remembers several gold mines still working in the nearby hills, at Capleston (named after Irish prospector Patrick Caples) and Boatman's Creek.

Terry Young tells me in 2014 that he owned and ran a gold mine here for some years but closed it in the mid-1990s. His farm borders the vanished gold boom town of Capleston. He helped with a Department of Conservation archeological dig there and was fascinated with the relics of life in the 1800s that the work party unearthed.

Gold towns proliferated on the West Coast. Their names are inscribed in local history as in a roll of honour. Many are hard to find today. When you do find them, there is often little to see. Such a town is Notown, in the Lower Grey Valley.

People sometimes ask me, "Did Notown really exist?" I knew it must have existed because a sign on the church at Shantytown says the building was first used at Notown, before removal to Ngahere and then to Shantytown.

In 2010, I drive up a narrow valley to find the place. The public road ends at a stream and by the time you get there you have seen nothing but bush, scrub and hills.

Then you spot a sign that points to the cemetery. I go in there and look around. It is a tidy little graveyard where the remains of maybe 50 to 100 people were laid to rest. That is evidence enough for me. Notown was a yes-town.

My visit to Waiuta is a little different. But then, Waiuta was a very different place. This gold town, high on a plateau behind Reefton, appeared late on the scene. Its gold was deep and hard to reach so mining here required huge investment. This happened at last in 1908 when British firm Consolidated Goldfields Ltd formed a subsidiary, Blackwater Minerals. The new company poured money into establishing a town at Waiuta and launching a major mining operation. Waiuta then became the West Coast's wealthiest mine in the 20th century.

Then, in 1951, a shaft collapse and falling gold prices prompted the company to close the mine and move out. The loss of jobs was catastrophic for the substantial town of some 500 people. They too moved out. Waiuta died overnight.

Learning of this intrigues me and I want to know more. So, in 2008, I drive through Ikamatua and take the right-turn up Waiuta Road. After a climb through bush so dark that signs ask you to turn your headlights on, I emerge on a large patch of mown ground where the Department of Conservation has erected information signs.

Four cottages still stand but no one seems at home. A large building, formerly the hospital, is a Bible camp. No one is there. I am alone, with no one to interview about Waiuta. It is annoying to think I won't be able to write a Heartland column about this place, but I can't just invent information. So I head back down the hill and head for Runanga instead, where I hope to find an old identity to talk to about coal mining.

The place to look for such a character is the Workingmen's Club. Sure enough, an elderly gent is standing at the bar with an almost empty beer glass and too few coins left to fill it again.

I ask him if he is from Runanga.

"Nah," is the reply.

I ask him where he is from then.

"Waiuta," he says.

I offer him a beer. And soon he is telling me all I could ever have wanted to know about the deserted village on the hill.

He is Tony Mangan and he says his family was the last to leave Waiuta, in 1951. He was 12 then and he remembers life there vividly. He talks of school, the swimming baths, playing rugby (I noticed the goal posts were still standing), tennis on asphalt courts, movies in the hall on Saturday night, the resident policeman keeping the peace around the hotel, rare trips by Road Services bus to the "big-smoke" of Greymouth. There was a good range of shops, other businesses and state services, he says.

The picture Mangan presents is of a self-sufficient town – and perhaps the most sudden death any New Zealand town ever suffered.

I ask him where his family moved to.

"Denniston," he says.

Rusting relics, ghost towns, faded memorials in cemeteries … but what strikes me as much about West Coast gold mining is that it has never quite died. Fossickers still do a bit of hobby panning, of course, as they do in parts of Central Otago. But larger scale mining continues too. I see it at places as far apart as Ross, Blackwater (in the Upper Grey Valley) and Globe Hill (east of Reefton).

Gary Ewing, an executive with mining company OceanaGold, has information to share with me for a Heartland column on Reefton. I drive over the Lewis Pass and meet him at the Globe Hill mine in 2014.

Ewing has a fascinating story to tell about brewer Stewart Monteith who landed in Dunedin in 1863, at the height of the Otago gold rush. He set up a brewery in Dunedin but left the town after a brush with the law over liquor licensing matters. He next established the Phoenix Brewery in Reefton in 1868, during the height of the West Coast gold rush. Monteith died at Reefton in 1921. His name survives in Greymouth's Monteiths Brewery, now a subsidiary of national brewing company DB.

Below: At Waiuta the burnt-out remains of a house do not symbolise the fate of the town. For Waiuta was not burnt-out. The substantial town was dismantled in the 1950s when gold mining ceased. An eerie feeling strikes the visitor to this deserted high plateau south of Reefton.

Above: Relicts of gold mining and a few old cottages remain at Waiuta. The substantial town was dismantled in the 1950s when mining ceased. An eerie feeling strikes the visitor to this deserted high plateau south of Reefton.

Below: Gary Ewing used to wonder what became of the headstone from brewer Stewart Monteith's grave. Now he wonders where this new headstone came from. Ewing was annoyed that only a crumbled fragment of Monteith's original headstone could be found after the Reefton Pioneers Cemetery was cleared. His view was expressed in a Heartland column in *The Press*. Then this headstone appeared.

Unfortunately his name does not survive at his burial place, Reefton's Pioneer Cemetery. Many headstones here were broken or lost over the years and the cemetery was converted into a park. Ewing found a chunk of stone with the letters -NTEITH legible at the top, as he was walking his dog through the park one evening. The segment has been identified as part of Monteith's headstone.

Ewing wants to have the headstone restored and has a Greymouth stonemason lined up for the job. What about the cost? Ewing hopes DB will fund the project as a memorial to a notable gold rush character who features in DB's advertising.

I love the story but am equally impressed by the scale of the open cast mine at Globe Hill. Ewing shows me around, on condition that I take no photographs. So I print on my mind a vision of a massive hole in the mountain that makes huge earthmoving trucks look like ants.

The restriction on photos is lifted when Ewing shows me historical gold mining items the company has salvaged from the site and arranged as a display for interested visitors.

Another display of old mining gear stands beside the Blenheim-Nelson highway, a little south-east of Havelock. For many passing travellers it is the first inkling they have that Marlborough ever had a gold rush.

In the same year that the West Coast gold rush started, a discovery in Marlborough drew 6000 miners there. Gold in Otago and Southland, gold in Westland and Buller, gold in Nelson and Marlborough – the 1860s was a golden era indeed for the South Island.

The Marlborough display was set up in 1964 as a centennial memorial to the prospectors who rushed to the Wakamarina River area when news reached them that gold had been discovered there.

Hundreds of prospectors' tents quickly spread across the small plain where the highway

now crosses the river. The settlement gained the appropriate name of Canvastown. The tents have gone now but the name remains. The Trout Hotel is the only living relic.

In the hotel in 2013, I meet publican Raymond Cresswell. He says the old pub keeps going, while country pubs elsewhere are struggling, because of a strong community spirit among the farming and forestry folk. This spirit, he says, has grown out of a pride in the area's history.

All the locals know the story of a young pioneer woman, Mrs Pope, who was doing the family wash in the Wakamarina River in 1860. She noticed specks of gold on the clothes and talked about it openly. This stirred some interest and a few prospectors began poking around.

Four years later a prospector made a payable strike. The big rush followed. An estimated two tonnes of gold was dug out in the first year.

The profitable diggings were in the hills a few kilometres up river from Canvastown but the settlement prospered as a supply base because of its location on the road from Blenheim and the port of Havelock. Cresswell says five pubs once operated here. The Trout is the lone survivor. Attached to it are two new motel units that are popular with visiting anglers. Near it are a former shop, a former church that is now a house, and the old hall. A new fire station completes the picture.

Over the river is the rugby ground. Canvastown has no senior grade team now but Cresswell treasures memories of senior matches played there and the players of both teams using the hotel for changing rooms and after-match drinks.

So Canvastown may have another claim to fame – the only location where senior rugby players had to cross a state highway bridge to get from changing room to playing field and back again.

Above: The name Canvastown suggests a place covered in tents. Resident Raymond Cresswell explains this river flat between Blenheim and Nelson was once a tent town. Gold was discovered in the river and diggers swamped the place. Today his Trout Hotel hosts anglers, farm and logging workers – and travellers wondering what the name means.

Logging and sawmilling helped sustain Canvastown after gold mining petered out. But the advent of large truck and trailer units that could transport logs on good roads to mammoth mills in the big towns ended that respite for Canvastown. It has slowly declined since the 1950s.

Even bigger than Canvastown was Cullensville, a gold town at the foot of the Richmond Range, near Linkwater, halfway along the Queen Charlotte Drive between Picton and Havelock. A gold strike in Cullen's Creek in 1888 started a rush here.

Local farmer John Collins says 2000 people lived at Cullensville at its peak from the late-1880s to the end of the century. It had a stately main street along which stood 32 business premises, including three "licensed establishments".

Collins' roots are here, he tells me in 2013. His forebears dug for gold. He still digs for gold. He shows me a bottle half-filled with flakes and lumps of gold he panned from old quartz tailings at Cullensville.

After diggers began panning for gold in the streams, gold-bearing quartz reefs were found in the hill higher up. Mining of the quartz boosted Cullensville. A five kilometre-long aerial ropeway was erected and brought the gold-bearing rock to a large stamper battery near the town. There the rock was crushed and the gold extracted.

Above: A gravel road leading into bush-clad hills hardly looks significant. But up this road once sat the bustling town of Cullensville. Gold made the town and the end of gold spelled the end of the town, just south of Linkwater in the Marlborough Sounds area.

Cullensville, in all its glory, lasted little more than a decade. Gold-bearing ore became more difficult to find from the mid-1890s. This made the stamper battery uneconomic and it closed. Most of the workers and miners and their families left the district. Collins smiles as he adds that a few departures might have been hastened by fires that destroyed two of the three hotels.

A few diggers remained though. They scratched a living. Their numbers swelled when unemployed men arrived in the Depression.

Collins' parents married here in the Depression. His father could not afford to buy a wedding ring so took some gold he had panned to a jeweller who made it into a ring to place on his bride's finger. Collins still has that ring.

Collins bought 500 hectares of old gold workings at Cullensville in 1964 for "a pound an acre". He fossicked over it for years before selling it again. As well as finding gold, he came across lead pellets from shot guns and bones from large birds. He concludes from this that the miners hunted native pigeons for food.

He dug up many old bottles from the site of a cordial factory, and traces of Chinese market gardens just outside the former town.

Over the hill from Cullensville were further quartz reefs bearing gold. Here the gold town of Waikakaho enjoyed a similarly brief boom time. However, it was not as productive and became known as a "poor man's gold field".

Collins says the twin towns were just close enough for their rugby teams to climb over the range, beside the 1055-metre-high Mt Cullen, and play against each other. It was a tough climb so the weary visitors must have conceded a considerable amount of what is known today as "home-town advantage". To rub it in further, the losing team had to pay for "supper" for both teams at a local pub after each match.

Local historian Cynthia Brooks has collected many yarns, anecdotes and photographs of Waikakaho in her book, *The Calm Beyond*. One story tells of pioneers Joseph Wratt and his wife, Mary.

Joseph had left home in Nelson after arguing with his father. This, and jobs in farming, sawmilling, fencing and railway construction, might have concerned Mary's devout Methodist father when the young couple decided to marry. Mary, only 17, was many months pregnant, which probably supported his view.

Joseph and Mary farmed on land they leased from local Maori at Waikakaho. There they had 15 children. The first was born the day after their wedding. Three of the children died young.

The Wratts wrung a living from Waikakaho's soil for a decade before the gold rush, and for another decade after. They showed that miners were not the only characters sentenced to a lifetime of hard yakka in the gold fields.

But they survived, even to the extent that descendants of Joseph and Mary still farm in the district.

Below: Cullensville, south of Linkwater in the Marlborough Sounds area, still offers reminders of its golden past, when hundreds of miners sought their fortune. It was a short-lived search.

CHAPTER 9

Warriors of the South

A YOUNG MAORI SOLDIER kneels by a grave. His arms embrace the headstone. His head is bowed. His eyes drizzle tears that drip from his chin.

The New Zealand fern is inscribed on the white headstone. The grave is one of 1100 that contain the remains of New Zealanders, among those of other Allied nations in the Commonwealth War Graves Cemetery at El Alamein, in the Egyptian desert.

When I pass through the impressive portal and catch my first sight of the cemetery spread before me, my heart breaks at the sight. Row upon row of graves indicate where so many of our men lie. And I think, this "foreign field" is as much a part of our heartland as any South Island town, from Owaka to Collingwood.

That explains why, of all the 500 Heartland columns, only one is based outside New Zealand. El Alamein is it, and I make no excuses.

The soldier at the grave is part of a Maori cultural group that is in El Alamein in 2012 to mark the 70th anniversary of the battles here in World War II. The cultural group has accompanied 24 veterans of the North Africa Campaign to revisit the battlefield, courtesy of the NZ Defence Force. I am travelling with them to report on the event for the Fairfax newspapers in New Zealand.

After the official ceremonies of remembrance, we are given an hour to move independently around the vast cemetery where New Zealanders' graves occupy about a quarter of the space. This is when I spot the young soldier. I stand back to allow him space to express his grief and his unity with, perhaps, a member of his whanau who never came home.

As I move away, the sun is setting over the desert, the air is cooling, people are shuffling back towards the portal and, from the mosque in the nearby town, a voice is calling Muslims to prayer.

It is the sort of atmosphere that prompts reflection. I cast eyes over our veterans' contingent. It includes six South Islanders: Tom McNabb of Owaka in South Otago, Andy McGovern from Timaru, Huia Holmes and Verdun Affleck, both of Geraldine in South Canterbury, Bill Leitch of Greymouth and Maurice Abrahams of Nelson.

What can it mean to these men and their North Island buddies? I search their faces for an answer. They look grim, yet a hint of

Opposite: The killing fields: The monument north of Kaiapoi marks the site of Kaiapoi Pa where northern chief Te Rauparaha's warriors laid siege to the local Ngai Tahu people, before attacking and overcoming them. Only a few Ngai Tahu escaped.

resignation shows they have accepted the past and moved on. They mourn inwardly though. Watch their eyes, their mouths. There is a hint of wistfulness – perhaps even discomfort – that they are here, hale and hearty in their 90s, while the mates they remember died before they even had a life.

Some of our party have found the graves of old friends. Some old comrades will never be found. Dotted among the 1100 are headstones engraved with the words: "A soldier of the war, 1939-1945, 2NZEF, Known unto God". Stark acknowledgement that the barbarity of war has caused such mutilation as to prevent identification of some bodies.

What can it mean to the veterans' families? In the cemetery I meet Andy McGovern's daughter Jo and granddaughter, Louise. They have travelled all this way to meet up with Andy and share these special moments with him. They tell me he has been looking forward to this trip enormously. He was determined to make it. He knows it will be his last.

It reminds me of watching old Christchurch soldier Jack Cummins as he laid poppies on the graves of three mates in a Commonwealth cemetery at Florence, Italy, in 2009. I took his elbow as he, gripping his stick, rose slowly and said simply to his departed mates, "I don't think I'll be back".

Heading back through the cemetery at El Alamein, towards the portal, I see a couple who just have to be New Zealanders. I ask them where they are from. They say Greymouth.

They are Matt and Linda Lysaght. They have come to Egypt to join a guided tour of the battlefields of World War II. Each had an uncle who fought here. They say it is important to remember the sacrifice made by all who fought, those who came back and those who didn't.

Below: Return of the Kiwis: Nelson man Maurice Abrahams fought in the North Africa campaign of World War II. Along with 24 other veterans, he visited El Alamein in 2012. After commemoration services the men looked for graves of old comrades in the New Zealand section of the Commonwealth War Cemetery.
Abrahams family collection

What can it mean to old foes, the Germans and Italians whom our men opposed in the desert so long ago? I ask former parachutist Valentino De Bortoli of Italy's elite Lightning (Folgore) Division. In faltering English he answers: "We are friends now". He repeats it twice as if to reinforce the sentiment.

De Bortoli has one arm around New Zealander Norman Leaf. The veteran from our party speaks for both of them as he adds: "Many of the Italians did not want to fight. The average Italian is just a normal person. The old enmity is gone. But the sadness is always there".

The coach taking us back to our hotel stops at the Italian and German war memorials a few kilometres outside the town of El Alamein. In each huge edifice the victims of war were buried in a common grave. Their names are on plaques that line the walls – tens of thousands of plaques. For each plaque I see in my mind a grieving family in Italy or Germany when news of a loved one who is dead reaches them. They look just like grieving families in Winton or Tapawera. Certainly, the pain of loss knows no borders.

And what do the Egyptians think of all this? As we leave the cemetery and walk the 70 metres to our bus, we have to weave through a protest group of local people. I ask them what they are protesting about and they tell me of the thousands of unexploded land mines the Allied armies left behind in the sand and the horrible injuries that still occur when people unwittingly step on one. They want our governments to clean up this mess.

Above: The battles at Alamein were the Allies' first major victory on land and a turning point in World War II. New Zealand troops played key roles in the fighting. When the German withdrawal gained pace, these Kiwis had a chance to relax for a while.
Syd Hallett

As we drive back through the town we pass the war museum that we visited the day before. It is dated and a little shabby but still quite an attraction to a town that has little else to interest tourists.

There was no town here before the war, just a railway siding. I remember our visit to the railway station yesterday. I will never forget the faraway look on our veterans' faces as they stood outside the forlorn little station building and gazed into infinity.

New Zealand is a peaceful country, yet war has often been with us. This has been brought home to me by 25 years of interviews with veterans of wars, men who fought from Gallipoli to Vietnam. The point is made even more graphically by a walk through the former Kaiapoi Pa with Ngai Tahu historian Te Maire Tau in 2007.

A tall white monument near State Highway 1 between Woodend and Waikuku in North Canterbury marks the spot. A major Ngai Tahu pa stood on gently sloping ground here. It was a prime trading centre in pounamu brought from the West Coast rivers. Maori canoes carried traders up a stream from the mouth of the Ashley River.

However, Te Rauparaha's Ngati Toa warriors did not paddle up this stream to launch their 1831 attack on the pa. They landed further north, near present-day Amberley, and approached Kaiapoi overland. They laid siege to the pa while they waited for their moment. Then, when they were ready, the invaders stormed the ramparts and broke through the walls of the pa.

A terrible massacre ensued, says Tau. When it ended, 1000 bodies lay dead. Only a handful of Ngai Tahu managed to escape. They fled south, taking word of the bloody event to kinfolk in settlements along the coast as far south as Temuka.

Tau points out half-lost features of the old pa as we walk over the site, about the area of five football fields. Here were huts, there gardens. That marshy strip overgrown with rushes was a flowing stream. This long hump was part of the earthen ramparts. He indicates where gates stood – there, there, and there.

This is a place to stand and reflect on New Zealanders' willingness to go to war – a willingness that persisted for another 150 years after the fall of Kaiapoi Pa.

An urge for utu (revenge) brought the great southern Ngai Tahu chief Tuhawaiki up to Kaiapoi and on to Wairau (Marlborough) to satisfy iwi honour with a victory over Te Rauparaha.

Then what happened? A monument on a hill between the Southland towns of Mataura and Wyndham provides the answer.

It was here, in 1837, that a Ngai Tahu war party under Tuhawaiki defeated a raiding party of North Island Ngati Tama warriors, under chief Te Puoho.

Victory for the southerners on this low hill at Tuturau, by the eastern bank of the Mataura River, has great significance. It heralded the end of inter-tribal wars in the South Island.

Te Puoho had embarked on this crusade confident of success even though Te Rauparaha had cautioned against it. After landing their canoes near the future site of Nelson, the invaders had marched down the West Coast, through the Haast Pass and across Southland to this point. They had overrun opposition in small skirmishes, sacking villages and pillaging food supplies along the way. But they would meet a grisly end at Tuturau.

I climb the slope to the monument in 2012 and peer over the surrounding countryside. In my imagination I am a lookout at the Tuturau Pa. I see some far-off shapes that must be fugitives from Te Puoho's approach. They are fleeing to Bluff where they will raise the alarm. I fancy that blur to the south is the war party that

Tuhawaiki has quickly raised, moving silently to surround Te Puoho's men as they sleep.

The invaders, smug after their conquests so far, settled down for a night of much needed sleep. They awoke suddenly, to be met by fit and fresh warriors from the south who routed them. Many of Te Puoho's men were killed. Others were taken as slaves for Tuhawaiki.

Thus did the northern chief's ambition to seize the southern land of Murihiku (Southland) die. And thus did the shedding of blood in South Island inter-tribal conflicts end – forever.

That seems a long time ago but European history in New Zealand is short. Even before the North Island raiders approached the Tuturau hill, Pakeha whaling boats were already working from the Aparima River lagoon, the site of Riverton, on the Southland coast.

Tuturau farmer Don Hesselin told me about the battle in 1970. Hesselin's father had been involved in the erection of the Tuturau monument in 1937. Hesselin's grandfather could have been a lad at Riverton when Te Puoho's men marched down the South Island in 1836-1837. Look at it that way and it does not seem so long ago.

The Tuturau monument is plain, almost unattractive. It is unseen by most people because it stands above a back road. It was erected in the Depression to mark the centenary of the battle. Lack of funds at that time, and possibly lack of interest in things Maori, might have dictated the simplicity of the structure but it seems a pity that such a moment in South Island history should receive such scant recognition.

Then I remember another monument. Just south of Timaru a sign by State Highway 1 points down Scarborough Road to the Tuhawaiki Monument. I drive down there in 2008 and meet local farmer (and 1958 All Black loose forward) Tom Coughlan.

A rugged stone cairn with a plaque is set in a corner of native trees about 300 metres up from the coast. Coughlan says it marks the place, on the rocks below, where Tuhawaiki drowned in 1844. He was thought to be only 40 years old.

Below left: Intertribal wars in the South Island ended here, at Tuturau, near Mataura in Southland. The monument marks the place where southern Ngai Tahu chief Tuhawaiki's war party attacked and vanquished Te Puoho's Ngati Tama invaders in 1836.

Below right: Tuhawaiki was a great southern chief of Ngai Tahu. From his base on Ruapuke Island in Foveaux Strait, Tahuwaiki led the raid that ended intertribal warfare in the South Island. He drowned when his ship foundered just south of Timaru. This monument stands near the point where he died.

Coughlan and his wife, Jane, researched Tuhawaiki's importance to history and decided to cut a piece off their property for the monument. Local iwi agreed to help with the project. Beside the Tuhawaiki cairn are two smaller stones representing the Ngai Tahu people who owed so much to this mighty warrior.

The Coughlans tell me Tuhawaiki mixed freely with European whalers down south. They taught him English and agriculture. They converted him to Christianity, showed him how to handle boats and educated him in the art of swearing.

Tuhawaiki was sailing up the coast when he steered towards shore to collect fresh water. A freak wave washed him overboard and he was unable to save himself. His body was buried first at Arowhenua, north of Timaru. It was then disinterred for reburial on his home ground of Ruapuke Island, in Foveaux Strait.

A quite different monument stands on a hillside at Tuamarina, north of Blenheim. The significance of this structure is not so much related to a war, as to the avoidance of a war.

The incident at Tuamarina was once called the Wairau Massacre. Now it is known as the Wairau Affray. What happened in this northeast corner of Marlborough's Wairau plain in 1843 aroused powerful emotion among European settlers. But it was far from the one-sided slaughter that the word "massacre" implies.

Maori-Pakeha relations were becoming strained over land issues, especially in the North Island, just three years after the signing of the Treaty of Waitangi.

Meanwhile, immigrants were pouring into the new colony of Nelson. They wanted good farm land and they were prepared to trample over Maori rights guaranteed in the treaty, to get their hands on Wairau's fertile plain.

I explore the site in 2007 and am more taken by the ancient titoki tree that stands beside the Tuamarina Stream, below the Blenheim-Picton highway, than by the monument on the hill above.

The monument bears the names of the 22 Europeans who were killed, some by execution, in the affray. The titoki tree was there when the event happened. It was already about 15 years old. Around its branches resounded the blasts of musket fire and the screams of men dying in violence. If a tree could talk …

At the Tuamarina Primary School I ask principal Neil Chalmers what local school pupils think about this event. He says his senior classes do a research study on the issue every two years. A summary of the findings of one group's study appears on a sign that stands at the site.

The sign says Ngati Toa had controlled this land from 1827 and had extended hospitality to European settlers. However, Ngati Toa specifically banned any surveying of the land by Europeans. When New Zealand Company surveyors started surveying, the Maori pulled their survey pegs out of the ground. The surveyors left and returned to Nelson in frustration. The Maori burned their huts to deter them from coming back.

The NZ Company, which was in charge of colonising Nelson, decided to teach the Maori a lesson. They assembled a party of 49 armed men, who returned to Tuamarina. A stand-off between Maori and Pakeha followed, as the opposing groups lined either side of the stream and argued the case.

A small group of NZ Company men then crossed the stream and, as debate heated up, a musket went off, it is thought by accident. The shot sparked some shooting, from which four Europeans and three Maori soon lay dead. The fighting escalated until the Europeans were forced to retreat up the hillside to where the monument now stands. There they surrendered.

Among the dead was a high-ranking Maori woman, Te Rongo, wife of Chief Te

Rangihaeata. According to Maori custom, this death demanded utu. This was exacted with the execution of some Europeans, increasing their death toll to 22. It is not known how many Maori died.

Nelson's settlers were furious at the outcome of the Wairau expedition. They were even more furious at the result of New Zealand Governor Robert FitzRoy's judicial ruling on the matter. FitzRoy exonerated the Maori for their action, judging that they had been provoked by the settlers' actions, which had been in breach of the treaty.

Chalmers says the original Tuamarina School was built in 1871 on the very site of the executions. The school was moved a few years later to allow excavations for roading improvements. It is said a musket believed to have been used in the affray was dug up in the excavations – a gripping memento to motivate the pupils in their study.

Apart from the senseless actions, arguments and losses of life at Tuamarina, I feel the greatest significance of the affray is that it spelt the end of Maori-Pakeha hostilities in the South Island. While the New Zealand Land Wars raged in the North, the people of the South got on with life – and with one another. In future wars Maori and Pakeha would fight together for their country.

War memorials interest me and one I find in the Motueka district in 2012 is special. Just off the road that skirts the Motueka River is the tiny village of Ngatimoti. It is not much more than a school, a church, a hall, a golf course and a war memorial, set in the beautiful Orinoco Valley.

The inscription on the memorial tells me that local farm worker William Ham was "the first New Zealander to fall" in World War I. Private Ham died of wounds at the Egyptian town of Ismailia on February 5, 1915.

Below: Lest we forget: Private William Ham, a farm worker from Nelson's Motueka Valley, was the first soldier serving in the New Zealand Army to be killed in World War I. This monument to him and other local men who served dominates the peaceful scene at the tiny village of Ngatimoti, above the Motueka River.

It is staggering to think that a place of such serene charm as Ngatimoti could have produced this country's first victim of a world war. When I quote the inscription in a Heartland column, several readers email me to say it is wrong. They cite a New Zealander who was killed before Ham. So I do some research and find they are technically correct. However, the earlier victim, though born and raised in New Zealand, had shifted to Australia before the war and joined the Australian army at the outbreak of hostilities. There may have been others such before Ham.

What we can be sure of is that Ham was the first soldier serving in the New Zealand Army to be killed in action during World War I.

The battle by the Suez Canal, near the town of Ismailia, came two months before the infamous Gallipoli Campaign. New Zealand troops training near Cairo were ordered to move north urgently by train as observer aircraft had spotted a Turkish force 12,000-strong advancing on the Suez Canal, clearly with intention of taking control of it.

The New Zealanders were to reinforce Indian Army units defending the canal. The ensuing battle quickly swung in the Allies' favour and the Turks were forced to withdraw – but not before a bullet had struck Ham in the neck, breaking his spinal column. He was taken to Ismailia Hospital where he died two days later.

Ham must have been among the first to enlist in the army for World War I. He sailed from New Zealand by troopship scarcely two months after Britain's declaration of war – time that included army training at Christchurch's Addington Show Grounds.

It is likely he was encouraged by a neighbour, Cyprian Brereton. In peace time Brereton, a Ngatimoti farmer, had been an officer in the "part-time" army. At the start of the war he was put in command of the Nelson Company which formed part of the Canterbury Battalion. He knew Ham personally and oversaw his burial at Ismailia.

The Ngatimoti memorial lists 12 other local men who were killed in that war – two at Gallipoli and 10 on the Western Front.

Local school principal Ali Turner tells me Ngatimoti is "a piece of paradise". It must have felt like "Paradise Lost" when 13 fine sons of this close-knit community failed to return from the war.

Much has been written about the battles of World War I but little about the horses that served behind the scenes. This neglect has long irked North Canterbury horsewoman Theresa Rosanowski. She called me in 2014 and suggested a Heartland column could do something to redress the balance.

I visit Rosanowski and she delivers some surprising statistics about the transport roles that New Zealand horses filled in "The Great War". The most stunning figures are:

- 10,000 – the number of horses that New Zealand shipped abroad for service in the war.
- 4 – the number of horses that returned.
- 3 – the number of memorials to the war horses in New Zealand.

Our tough farm horses were ideally suited to the hardships and rigors of war, Rosanowski says. They hauled men, guns, ammunition, food and medical supplies, machinery, timber, iron … the list goes on.

They endured desert sand storms and sunstroke in Egypt and Palestine, deep mud and waterlogged shell holes in France and Belgium. They became tangled in barbed wire, pierced by shot and shell, obliterated by bombs tossed from planes. Equine flu killed 75 New Zealand horses. Colic and poisoning disabled many.

Some of the horses were sold at war's end. Some were "put down" to prevent their being obtained by potentially cruel masters. So, it is unknown how many survived. The four that came home were the personal steeds of senior New Zealand Army officers. Rank and privilege.

Rosanowski takes me to Birch Hill Station, near Okuku at the north-west edge of the Canterbury Plains. Here stands one of the country's three memorials to the horses of war. She explains that station owner Edward Milton combined the running of the station with his career as a senior officer in the territorial army early last century. Milton buried his military horse Kakahu, on the station, and established a private cemetery here.

The horse memorial stands in the cemetery. The plaque on it reads: "In memory of the horses of the 8th Regiment of NZMR (NZ Mounted Rifles) that died in the Great War, 1914-1918".

To mark the centenary of the war, in 2015, Rosanowski organised a mass ride-in for a service of remembrance of the horses. Riders from all over Canterbury took part, with army personnel and community representatives joining in the service and associated events.

It was a great success, says Rosanowski. But she would still like to see more recognition of the horses of war, all around the country.

Left: They also served: This monument at Birch Hill station in North Canterbury honours the 10,000 New Zealand horses that served with our troops in World War I. Only four horses returned to their homeland after the war.

Above: Ted's bottle is still waiting for his return. Waihao Forks, South Canterbury, publican Shane Doolan, says the bottle attracts visitors who have been moved by the story of farmhand Ted D'Auvergne who said he would drink the beer when he got back from World War II. He was killed in Crete.

THE TALE OF THE MAN who left a bottle of beer on the bar to drink when he came back from the fighting may be the South Island's best known war story.

I call at the Waihao Forks Hotel, in pleasant rolling country behind Waimate, in 2014. Knowing that the story of Ted D'Auvergne has been written and published many times, I am seeking a new angle. Perhaps the publican can speak about the way the story has increased visitor numbers to this plain-looking country pub.

But first the story. Opposite the hotel you can see traces of the former Waimate railway branch line, station and stock yards. The line ran as far up-country as Waihao Downs, about four kilometres further inland.

D'Auvergne, a 34-year-old local farmer nicknamed Froggy because of his French descent, had enlisted in the army for service in World War II. He had orders to report to Burnham Military Camp, near Christchurch, to prepare to embark for service overseas in 1940. He walked down to the Waihao Forks village and, being a little early for the train, popped into the pub for a beer. Or two.

He had just bought a second bottle when the train whistle sounded, signalling that the train had left Waihao Downs and was on its way to the Forks. So D'Auvergne left the bottle unopened on the bar. He told the publican to keep it for him and they would drink it when he came back. And, of course, he never did.

That bottle, of Natural XXXX Beer, brewed by the Christchurch firm of Ballins, now stands protected in a glass case above the bar. Does it attract many tourists, I ask co-proprietor Sandy Doolan?

Her reply is an unequivocal "yes". Not only do locals frequent the pub and keep an eye on the bottle, many bring visitors here from all over the world. Crowds come from around South Canterbury every Anzac Day to raise a glass in honour of the man who never returned. Buses on club and group outings pull up at the door and disgorge their eager passengers. Campervans and caravans stop and a babble of strange accents accompanies the people who enter for a look – and hopefully a drink, Doolan adds.

All have heard the story and felt the poignancy of the soldier who left his farm and his beer to fight the foe, never to return.

Doolan tells me of a helicopter suddenly landing in the car park one day. Out stepped a smartly dressed Irishman who had read the story. He had been so touched he had flown to Christchurch and hired the chopper to bring him here. He entered the bar and announced in a strong brogue, "I want to see Ted's bottle".

His visit was worth a few double gins to the Waihao Forks Hotel, Doolan remembers fondly. But that was not the last she heard of the wealthy Irishman. A month later Doolan received a card from him in the post. He had gone to Crete, he wrote. He had found D'Auvergne's grave, there on the island where he and so many other Kiwis had been killed in the war.

Stewarts Gully is part of Christchurch now but it must have seemed "out in the wop-wops" during World War II. Tucked in behind flood banks that line the south bank of the Waimakariri River, it was a popular fishing spot where keen anglers built makeshift baches from the 1880s.

Probably typical of the building standard at that time was the construction David Rich describes in 2001. He remembers his father regularly biking 15 kilometres from Papanui northwards to Stewarts Gully. Tied onto his bike were lengths of timber, bits of corrugated iron, bags of nails, his saw and a tool box crammed with sundry implements. He would spend most of the day knocking bits and pieces together on his leased site at the gully. Then it was back on the bike for the ride home.

A kind of shantytown grew up at the gully, though the settlement contains more substantial homes now. In the Depression times of the 1930s it became a poor man's holiday resort and a popular destination for city excursionists with just sufficient funds to pay the return train fare.

But Stewarts Gully had its moment of glory. After Japanese planes bombed the American naval fleet at Hawaii's Pearl Harbour, in World War II, alarm spread throughout New Zealand. An attack on this country was feared. Some New Zealand Army units, nearing readiness for shipment to North Africa, were kept at home instead and sent to stiffen the defence of our beaches.

The huts and baches at Stewarts Gully were requisitioned to accommodate the 800 soldiers of the 1st Battalion, Canterbury Regiment, in 1942. Among them was Allan Hunter. To him the rustic huts seemed like palaces after enduring the discomforts of bell tents during training at Burnham.

The men were keen to fight and confident of repelling an enemy invasion, Hunter tells me in 2008.

"We would have put up a good show. We would not have surrendered."

The beaches to the east of Christchurch – New Brighton, North Beach, Waimairi and Spencerville – were a couple of hours march from Stewarts Gully. Hunter says much of the men's time was spent in marching there and back. At the beaches they prepared fortifications and kept watch out to sea for any sign of invasion craft.

Back at the camp they drilled on the tennis courts, shot at the target range, practised fieldcraft and radio skills in the forest, made route marches up long country roads, cleaned their gear and did their washing. Between-times they relaxed.

Hunter says some of the men devised ingenious ways of getting away from camp unnoticed and crossing the nearby railway bridge to visit the pubs in Kaiapoi. Sometimes friends left bikes hidden for them in the straggly willows that abounded along the riverside.

Sundays were open days when family and friends could come out on the train to visit the men in the camp. Some visitors were neither family nor friends, Hunter says with a knowing look. Remember, this was war time. Many men in their 20s were overseas and might never return. The young women of Christchurch were starved of male contact.

The American victory over the Japanese in the Battle of the Coral Sea turned the tide of war in the Pacific. The threat to New Zealand eased, helped also by thousands of US Marines arriving in the country for a break from the fighting. The "Yanks" spent their leave time with families who opened their homes to them. Many Canterbury farms became temporary havens for the Americans.

With the defenders no longer needed, the Stewarts Gully battalion was broken up. The men were posted elsewhere. Some served in Italy and the Pacific. Others were directed to work on farms and in essential industries around Canterbury.

Hunter switched to the navy. After peering from New Brighton sandhills at a watery horizon in search of ships, he was soon peering from a ship at glimpses of embattled Europe.

Above: Renowned landscape painter Austen Deans was badly wounded during fighting in Crete and spent the rest of World War II as a prisoner of the Germans. This gave him time to work at his art – including drawing fake identity papers for fellow prisoners attempting to escape.
David Hallett Fairfax Media NZ/The Press

Austen Deans did most of his fighting in World War II with a paint brush. Yet he began as a combat soldier, not an official war artist. I meet him twice in 2006, for Heartland columns on Burnham and Peel Forest.

At Burnham, Deans is among a group of 20th Battalion World War II veterans on a reunion trip around their old training ground of 1939. As their bus cruises around the military camp, I chat briefly with the man who has become a noted landscape water colourist.

With so many on board the bus, Deans cannot say much. As I leave the veterans, I feel hungry to learn more about him. Five months later I get my chance.

Peel Forest feels like a separate country – a sort of Duchy of the Bellbird. Its trill dominates the soft swish of occasional cars. The village sits in a timeless space near the Rangitata River but is closer to civilization than you can imagine.

And there, up on a hill, in the bush, accessible only by a stony track and the crossing of a tumbling creek, lives Deans. He is at home with rooms of paintings and windows with vistas of the Canterbury Plains to the far-off knobs of Banks Peninsula.

Deans enlisted early in World War II and served with the 20th (South Island) Infantry Battalion in Greece and Crete. He was wounded on the island of Crete and underwent surgery in an army dressing station. He regained consciousness in a cave system where wounded soldiers were laid for recovery. A couple of days later, the Germans overran the place and Deans was taken prisoner.

Because of the severity of his wounds, Deans was flown to a hospital on the Greek mainland, where he was given time to recuperate. He says conditions were difficult but he was able to scrounge paper and pencils and do some drawings. His artistic talent increased his ability to acquire materials. Soon he was using paint and brushes, working on portrait commissions for his guards and selling works to his fellow soldiers.

After several shifts, Deans was taken to a prisoner of war camp in Germany. He was still weak and was excused the hard labour that fellow prisoners had to do. Through the Red Cross he received parcels of art materials and his painting flourished. He produced dozens of works depicting life in the hospitals and camps. From memory he painted town and country scenes he had observed along the way.

Meanwhile, rather than trying to escape, he helped others by skilfully forging identification papers for them.

As Russian troops advanced on Germany late in the war, Deans was forced to join one of the horror marches in which thousands of Allied prisoners, poorly clad and weak from malnutrition and illness, trudged day after day through snow towards the West. Many did not survive. Deans did but many of his paintings were not seen again.

The paintings that eventually made their way home established Deans as an artist of importance. Belatedly he gained recognition as a war artist. His works have since rated a place beside those of Peter McIntyre and other appointed war artists.

It is easy to see in Deans' lined face and mischievous eyebrows why, after all this, he chose to settle and paint in the tranquillity of Peel Forest and take his inspiration from the South Island high country.

"I never found a nicer place to live. I found a rich and lovely community life here," he tells me in 2006.

Colin Brown has a similar love of the high country. He lives inland from Whitecliffs, on the banks of the Upper Selwyn River, west of Christchurch.

Whitecliffs was a small farming township that decayed through the latter 1900s. It is enjoying a renaissance now as a "getaway" for city folk seeking peace and quiet. Brown has seen much of its evolution, interrupted by the years he spent flying Hurricane and Spitfire fighter aircraft in World War II.

I visit the 90-year-old at his farm house in 2012. He says he still gets around the flatter paddocks, but only on a bicycle these days. The broken back he sustained in 1943 no longer allows him to stride the hills.

Naturally I ask him about his injury. He tells me he was based near Calcutta in India and making flights in a Spitfire to take reconnaissance photographs of bombing targets in Japanese-occupied Burma.

It was the monsoon season. Torrential rain storms were keeping Royal Air Force bomber squadrons grounded. At last a break in the weather prompted the order for Brown to take his plane up and get pictures of Japanese activities.

By the time he had flown the first stage of the mission, landed and refuelled for the second stage, thunder clouds were beginning to fill the sky. He took off again and was rapidly confronted by "half a dozen gigantic thunderstorms". He estimated the storm clouds rose to 40,000 feet in altitude.

Brown found a way around the storms and crossed over Burma, where he got his photographs. Then the trouble started. Brown suddenly became immersed in thick cloud. It bucked his plane about like a rodeo horse. The engine's carburettor froze, cutting the fuel supply. The plane went into a spin. Brown fought with the controls but the centrifugal forces were "violent". At 23,000 feet, in an unpressurised cockpit, he lost consciousness.

It must have been only seconds later that Brown awoke to find he was falling freely through the sky. He could see parts of his broken-up Spitfire dropping to earth near him. He tugged at the ripcord of his parachute and his fall was slowed. However, he was by then less than 3000 feet above the ground.

One good thing the monsoon did for him was make the ground sodden. Brown landed in shallow water. He felt numb. Only a little later did he feel the pain of a fractured spine. And later still did he calculate that he must have been in free-fall for at least 20,000 feet and survived. This was thought to be a then world record.

Brown says he loved flying Spitfires more than any other plane. He had other difficulties with them though. Once, returning from a mission to find the German battleship Tirpitz in Norway, with extra fuel tanks under the wings, the unbalanced plane clipped an oil drum on landing and crashed amid fears of a firestorm.

He flew again after that incident but not after his fall over Burma. He was packed in a plaster body cast for his long recovery.

Now he rides a bike around the paddocks at Whitecliffs. Aged 90!

Local RSA member Ian Evans tells me Brown commands enormous respect in the Malvern district. His presence at Hororata's annual Anzac Day parade attracts growing crowds each year.

Below: German forces were in retreat across North Africa after the battles at Alamein in World War II. These New Zealanders were among Allied troops who hounded and harried the enemy all the way to Tripoli.
Syd Hallett

CHAPTER 10

Power to the people

THE SOUTH ISLAND is as big as England but its population is equivalent to that of a second tier English city. So, with frequent rainfall, plentiful snow on the mountains to store water, a myriad of lakes and rivers, coal to burn, incessant winds and tides that surround us, we should never be short of electricity.

World War II caught us out. Our war effort put hydro dam construction on the back-burner for six years. Then the troops, the sailors, the flyers came home. They were young in years but prematurely aged. They wanted to put the war behind them and settle into normal lives. They married and triggered the baby boom.

Power cuts were a regular occurrence into the 1950s as rationing of electricity became necessary. Governments from then until the 1980s focussed on the building of dams to increase power output. A generation of workers spent their entire working life on power schemes. An itinerant workforce, and many families, moved from dams at Roxburgh to Benmore and Aviemore, and then to a succession of dams around Twizel, to Manapouri, to Clyde.

Electricity generation is a powerful theme in South Island history, in more ways than one. As I travel the heartland to gather ideas for *The Weekend Press* columns, I continually find examples of hydro schemes impinging on people's lives. Meeting Edna Capell at Lake Hawea in 2007 provides such a snippet.

The Hawea River flows from the lake and joins the Clutha River at Albert Town, just below Lake Wanaka. I had wondered about the function of the Lake Hawea outlet dam until Capell explained it.

The Ministry of Works set up a works camp where the present Lake Hawea village stands and built a dam on the outlet in the mid-1950s, she says. This was done so the outflow from the lake could be regulated and a steady flow of water to the Roxburgh Dam, then under construction, could be maintained.

Capell, from Dunedin, married Hawea rabbiter Tim in 1940. They settled into life in what was a remote spot, before completion of the Haast Pass highway that sweeps by the village. She remembers her husband's father running a fairly rudimentary guest house above the lake outlet. It catered mainly for anglers and hunters until Dunedin residents became increasingly mobile and began exploring the far reaches of Central Otago in the 1950s.

She and Tim took over the guest house and turned it into a hotel. They ran it until 1986, when they sold it. The village has grown beyond recognition even since then, she says. New

Opposite: Construction is under way on the Waitaki dam and power station in North Otago. Coinciding with the years known as The Slump, the hydro project was able to absorb many jobless men by using shovels and wheelbarrows instead of bulldozers and motor trucks.
Syd Hallett

housing subdivisions have sprung up. One is named Timsfield, after her late husband.

Dam building in the South Island dates back to well before World War II, of course. A story from the earlier periods that strikes me strongly is set deep in the Depression of the 1930s.

Jobless men were arriving every day at the Waitaki River Dam project. They came by bus, bike and foot from all over the country. They had heard there might be work available there. Job conditions in the barren, rocky place did not bother them. They were desperate for wages to send home so their families could eat.

Meanwhile, a small group of concerned citizens gathered around a kitchen table in Kurow, a farming township five kilometres below the dam site. They were moved by the plight of the straggling army of unemployed arriving daily in their midst. They would plan a "new deal" for New Zealand's working class.

The kitchen table was in Kurow's Presbyterian manse. Seated around the table were local Presbyterian minister Rev Arnold Nordmeyer, local GP Dr David McMillan, and others. These two would become Members of Parliament in the Labour Party's landslide election victory under Michael Joseph Savage in 1935. Nordmeyer would go on to serve as Minister of Finance in the one-term Labour Government of Walter Nash in the 1950s.

What had prompted these worthies to spend their time brainstorming ideas to improve the workers' lot? And did they have any idea how far-reaching would be the consequences of their planning? I find the answers while visiting Kurow in 2009, when men who worked on the Waitaki Dam scheme fill in some details for me.

Kurow had been a typical rural town, complete with railway branch line connecting to the main trunk just north of Oamaru. It stood on the south bank of the Waitaki River,

downstream from the rugged gorge where the dam was to be built.

Solid stone houses high above the point where the river emerges from the gorge were built as homes for the project chiefs. Still standing, they seem to proclaim the role the dam played in boosting the Kurow economy.

Construction of the dam began in 1929, after years of planning. When unemployment soared, the government made the choice to use the project as a relief scheme to soak up large numbers of unemployed.

"So, it was back to the days of the pick and shovel. It was barrows instead of bulldozers," one old-timer says.

By 1931 a camp more than twice the size of Kurow had sprouted for the workers. Strong winds buffeted the settlement on an exposed terrace above the river. Bunkhouses accommodated single men who slept on straw-filled sacks. Married men with families crammed into spartan wooden huts.

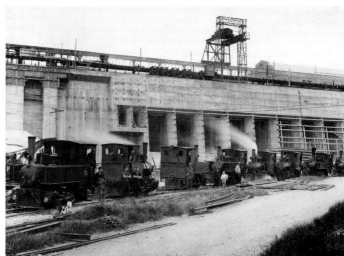

The population of the camp reached 3000, with wives and children making half of that number. On winter nights, they froze. On summer days, they baked. All year long, winds blew dust through every crack.

One of the bunkhouses was aptly named Siberia.

Working hours were long. The labour was arduous, especially for men unaccustomed to manual work. Pay was minimal. Many of the men sent it directly from the camp Post Office to wives back home to sustain the families they seldom saw.

Bruce Painters worked on the scheme. He says the high numbers of men arriving to ask for work played into the bosses' hands. Regulations, such as the ban on alcohol in the camp, were strictly enforced. Breaking any rule led to instant dismissal. There were few complaints and no strikes because anyone not working, or stirring trouble, could be easily replaced.

The men put up with working conditions that would not have been tolerated at other times. Minor injuries were common and horrific accidents occasional. Several deaths occurred. Long-term effects of working in freezing water and mud were suffered by many.

On the positive side, recreation rooms provided newspaper reading opportunity and library services, movies, billiards, cards, musical concerts by visiting groups and dances. Some workers even formed an orchestra.

The concerned citizens group that was meeting in the Kurow manse probably appreciated these measures to make life bearable in the camp. But the minister and the doctor had seen evidence of the working and living conditions that the men endured. They were shocked that fellow New Zealanders should be treated as these men were.

One practical outcome of the kitchen table discussions was the establishment of a health insurance system for the workers, funded from a levy on wages.

When they became MPs, Nordmeyer and McMillan adapted and extended this system into a proposed health and pensions plan for the whole country, to be funded from taxes. They pushed the plan through Parliament in their first term. The kitchen table discussions became embedded in the Social Security Act of 1938.

I turn my *Press* car away from Kurow and head up the Waitaki Valley. In a few minutes I pass the newer dams at Aviemore and Benmore. I cruise the streets of Otematata, the construction village for both these projects, and note how much more comfortable things were for workers here, some 30 years later.

Otematata is an attractive but quiet town. Once a hotel stop for bullockies and teamsters driving wagons up and down the valley, it blossomed from 1959 for construction of the Benmore Dam. Three thousand

Opposite above: Working conditions were harsh and the living was spartan on the Waitaki power scheme. But it did not deter thousands of unemployed men arriving on foot or bicycle seeking work here during the Depression. *Syd Hallett*

Opposite below: An extension to the railway enabled the shifting of heavy items brought from Oamaru to the Waitaki hydro project in the 1930s. *Syd Hallett*

dam workers and their families lived here until completion of the dam in 1965. Some stayed a while longer to work on the Aviemore Dam.

Then many of the houses were shifted to Twizel for workers on the Upper Waitaki hydro scheme. Otematata's permanent population dropped to below 200. Most of the houses that remain are owned by folk in Oamaru, Timaru and other places. They come for the fishing and boating – or just for the serenity.

Local resident Johnny Dalzell tells me Otematata relives its glory days over the Christmas-New Year holiday period. The population then swells to 3500.

Ian and June Rogers spent the early years of their marriage in a caravan at Otematata. June's father owned the earthmoving company W G Evans and Co which did contract work at Benmore from 1959 to 1962. Rogers worked on the giant machines while his wife cooked meals for the men.

Life in a caravan was difficult but memories of Otematata are pleasant for the couple. They recall sparkling frosts but say the town was lively and the community friendly. You could get everything you wanted here.

W G Evans operated the first Caterpillar D9 bulldozer in the South Island at Benmore. Ian says it and two Caterpillar scrapers worked alongside the machines of other contracting firms and the Ministry of Works, shifting gravel, clay and rock to form the core of the earth dam.

"It was a good work site. There was no dissension. Everyone helped each other," he says.

But he remembers one drawback – wind.

"The wind always blew. If it wasn't blowing down the gully, it was blowing up the gully. It was a cold job. In winter, the sun never reached the dam site."

Almost unceasing, the wind even stymied a plan to build an airstrip and fly DC3 aircraft in and out of Otematata with passengers and freight, Ian says.

Many dam workers moved to Twizel next, so I drive up there in 2013. Here I find a town that was built to be temporary but decided it wanted to be permanent.

Before irrigation brought swathes of green and herds of cows to parts of the Mackenzie Country, Twizel was an oasis in a desert. The well laid-out town was the base for the Upper Waitaki scheme.

The massive project that would link three lakes (Tekapo, Pukaki and Ohau) with rivers and canals for power generation at a string of four hydro stations ran from 1968 to 1985.

Twizel grew from its establishment in

1968 to a town more than twice the size of Otematata. It accommodated a hydro workforce of 6000, plus service workers, and families. It grew to become South Canterbury's second-largest town, exceeded only by Timaru.

After the project was completed, Twizel shrank. Then it set about re-establishing itself as a tourist town, conveniently situated near Aoraki-Mt Cook and halfway between Christchurch and Queenstown.

More than that, Twizel has developed its own attractions. Lake Ruataniwha, which was created as an add-on to the power project, has become the South Island's premier rowing and water sports venue. The hydro canals that slice through the parched plateau draw anglers by the dozen.

Malcolm Lousley is an enthusiast for Twizel. He moved here in 1971 to teach at the new high school. He has retired now but does some volunteer work for the local police.

Lousley remembers the town in its infancy. He has watched it grow, then decline, then sta-bilise, and now grow again.

The town was built of transportable houses, he tells me, so it could be moved to the Lower Waitaki (below Kurow) for the next big development scheme, which was then in the planning stage. When that scheme was abandoned, many of the workers were resent-ful. They had wanted to keep their community together. The shift downriver would have meant continued employment, which would have allowed that.

Instead, completion of the Upper Waitaki project spelled the end of Twizel's hydro community. The workforce broke up and most families moved away. Some houses were sold and shifted. But a group of locals who believed in Twizel's future decided to stay. Lousley was one of them.

Left: The charred hills of the Waitaki Basin make a sharp contrast with the turquoise water that flows from the Aviemore Dam. At this point the water is almost exhausted, with just one more power station to go.

Middle: And the first shall be last: The Waitaki Dam was the first built on the Waitaki River and became the last in a chain of eight generating electricity in the Mackenzie-Waitaki districts. Thousands of unemployed men found relief work building the dam during the Depression of the 1930s. Most of the work was done by hand.

Right: Benmore, the largest earth dam in New Zealand, was built on the Waitaki River between 1958 and 1965. Benmore followed construction of the Roxburgh Dam, on the Clutha River. Together they made a major contribution to solving the country's power crisis caused by the population surge after World War II and the increasing use of electrical appliances.

Above: The Clyde High Dam was built to a lesser height than planned. Its name was changed then to simply, the Clyde Dam. This followed protests against flooding the Cromwell Gorge and low-lying farm land north of Cromwell town, and fears that landslides blocking the newly formed lake could make the flooding worse. The dam still looks high if you are looking at it from Clyde and are of nervous disposition.

Below: Free at last, water that has been channelled from Lakes Tekapo, Pukaki, Ohau and Ruataniwha, and churned through three sets of turbines, is released near Twizel to pour into the Waitaki River. But its liberty will be short-lived because further dams and turbines lie ahead. Twizel identity Malcolm Lousley has seen the development of seven of the eight dams in the Waitaki scheme.

Opposite: High and dry above the flood, commercial buildings of old Cromwell are a visitor attraction. Much of the old town was flooded when the Clyde Dam was built downstream on the Clutha River. These buildings were dismantled and reconstructed higher up to form the Old Cromwell Town precinct.

He and a few other residents invested in some of the retail businesses and kept them afloat through dark times. Their confidence has been rewarded, he says. Tourism, dairying and salmon farming have brought a lift to the town.

Each day, as Lousley crosses the market square, he takes a count of the tourists and locals he sees. His home-made census shows tourists outnumber locals by five to one, on average.

"Twizel's future has come," he says.

Lousley shows me "flash new houses" that are going up around the town. One is owned by a wealthy Christchurch businessman who pops in and out by helicopter – such is the appeal of Twizel as a place to relax.

Other part-time residents arrive by car from the big towns and the cities. Twizel swells with people at holiday times. Tour coaches roll in and out continually. Now Lousley begins to fear Twizel may become like Queenstown and Wanaka – "where every second shop is a booze or food bar".

Twizel does not want to become Upper Wanaka, he laughs.

Lousley gives much of the credit for Twizel's rebirth to former hydro scheme engineer Max Smith. He was the visionary who, by wilful neglect of Wellington bureaucracy and judicious deployment of Ministry of Works personnel and machinery, created Lake Ruataniwha as a sports venue.

Smith was "a very gifted engineer", Lousley says. When plans and instructions came from Wellington, he amended them so they would work in Twizel's conditions. He stood up to the bosses and he won. He was so popular in Twizel that he was able to set rules for the town. These included bar closing times that ensured workers were on the job every morning, on time, and clear-headed.

"Max was a pragmatist. He made decisions and went with them. Head Office had to put up with it," Lousley says. "People didn't call him God for nothing."

Some of the Twizel workers did stay together, by moving to Cromwell for work on the Clyde Dam project. Cromwell, at the upstream end of the Cromwell Gorge, became a construction town for the dam at the downstream end of the gorge.

I visit Cromwell in 2014 and meet local identity Duncan Butcher. I ask him how the former Twizel workers got on in Cromwell. He shakes his head and says they might have wished they had not come.

Ministry of Works people were not liked and were not made welcome in Cromwell, says Butcher. He knows this first-hand, having been a Ministry of Works electrical overseer on the 1970s Clyde Dam project. He had come from Twizel earlier, via a stint at Manapouri.

Some local businesses refused to cash the ministry workers' cheques. Long-time residents resented the newcomers, many of whom were clever and able, for "taking over" in clubs and societies, he says.

Butcher traces the local people's antipathy to the government's decision to flood the much-photographed part of Cromwell that had appeared on many calendars, and to inundate farm land in the Upper Clutha Valley. This would have been the effect of building a "high dam" at Clyde. The dam's height was later reduced but the effect was still the creation of Lake Dunstan and the considerable flooding of parts of the area. The community's strong feeling persisted. It was manifest in the protest movement Power for the People.

Butcher says locals used to tackle him in the pub over Cromwell's grievance because he was a ministry man. He and his fellow workers copped the blame, he says. But he simply responded with the line: "I am a MOW [Ministry of Works] man. I am a project man. This is what I do. I build dams".

The ministry took measures to counter the negative impression. It agreed to develop Lake Dunstan as a recreational facility (perhaps influenced by the popularity of the unsanctioned Lake Ruataniwha). It identified

heritage buildings that would be flooded but were sound enough to be removed and re-sited above the water in the Old Cromwell Town heritage precinct.

In addition, the ministry undertook a "charm offensive". Using ministry equipment, staff built new swimming baths at the school and a new playground. They enlarged the existing 9-hole golf course to a full 18-hole course.

"That broke the ice," Butcher says. It made it easier for the hydro workers to stay. Which was just as well for Cromwell, as the men coming from Twizel were "hand-picked" for their ability to fit into the Cromwell community as well as for their professional expertise, Butcher says. The town has benefited from these workers, he adds.

Relationships improved so much that Butcher won election consecutively to the Cromwell Borough Council, the town's mayoralty, the Central Otago District Council and the Otago Regional Council.

As a ministry man he took no part in discussions on Cromwell's claim for compensation from the government over the drowning of part of the town. He cannot hide a smile, though, when recounting the town's success in these negotiations. The government provided Cromwell with $15 million worth of essential facilities, plus grants to sports bodies and contributions to a new shopping mall. Cromwell was to have paid back $5 million, over 25 years. However, when proposals for further dams in the gorge were dropped, Cromwell's debt was cancelled. The town had by then repaid just $300,000.

The post-World War II hydro dam trail from Roxburgh to Clyde and Manapouri lasted 30 years. It was and still is New Zealand's greatest era of large-scale new electricity generation. No large scheme has since got further than the drawing board. So what about the pre-war schemes?

So unexpected that it often features in quizzes is the fact that Reefton was the first town in New Zealand to bathe in the glow of electric street lighting.

Why Reefton? Why not? With the Inangahua River tumbling along parallel to the main street and a mere stone's throw from it, there was plenty of water to make a turbine spin.

I visit Reefton in 2011 and drive a couple of kilometres upriver to Blacks Point. There another surprise awaits me. A woman collecting her mail agrees to talk to me about this little former gold and coal mining town that travellers often think of as a suburb of Reefton. She introduces herself as Helen Bollinger.

It is a name I recognise through her work in television writing, presentation and production.

Why would she and her husband, Alun, also a TV personality, choose to live in this sleepy, dingy valley so walled-in by tall hills it seldom sees the sun for part of the year?

The reasons include family ties, warmth of community spirit among the 40 families and some of the best summers the Bollingers can remember anywhere in New Zealand. As for the winters – home is a snug 1874 weatherboard cottage that is warmed by a log fire.

A more striking reason, though, is Blacks Point's stirring history. The Bollingers settled here in the 1970s. That was a time when Reefton was awaking to its historic charm as a way to halt the town's decline. And nowhere were historical themes more concentrated than in Blacks Point.

Among the themes is the generation of electricity that powered Reefton's pioneering street lights. Bollinger shows me the concrete walls of the intake and water race, on the opposite bank of the Inangahua River. These diverted a strong flow from here to the power station in Reefton from as long ago as 1888.

When you think how some families in more "upmarket" parts of New Zealand did not get electricity for another half-century, you realise how forward-thinking Blacks Point and Reefton were in the heyday of gold and coal mining.

You might even say the women here were radical, to hear Bollinger tell of the Cornish miners' wives leading the charge for women's suffrage in 1890s' New Zealand. The Blacks Point Methodist Church hosted meetings of the Women's Christian Temperance Movement, which drove the suffrage cause forward. The Band of Hope played on the church steps to rally supporters to the cause.

New Zealand's male and misogynist establishment sneered at them, local miners scorned them over tankards in the Albion Hotel, but the women marched to victory.

How fitting that the former church now houses the excellent Blacks Point Museum.

Reefton must be among the earliest public power plants in New Zealand. It possibly inspired the people of Murchison to build a plant for their town and its surrounding dairy farming flats, some 40 years later.

The station was built six miles south of Murchison, which qualified it for the inspired name of Six Mile. Judy Peacock of the Murchison Museum finds some information on Six Mile for me and I drive there in 2012. Standing beside the road is the modest but well-preserved building that housed the generating equipment. A sign in front proclaims it as the oldest power station still existing in New Zealand. That is a proud claim, considering that the building withstood Murchison's tragic

Opposite: Love of history drew Helen Bollinger to live at Blacks Point, near Reefton. This walking bridge across the Inangahua River, near her home, leads to the intake where water was taken to power Reefton's hydroelectricity station from 1888. Reefton pioneered electric street lighting in New Zealand.

earthquakes of 1929. Evidence of the quakes is all around in landslips now covered with scrubby trees and bushes.

Six Mile generated electricity for 50 years from 1922. It was a small plant, producing 80 kilowatts, but it gave the local economy quite a boost. Electricians worked flat out connecting houses to the power lines. Farmers got electric machines installed in their milking sheds. This produced greater efficiency than hand milking and troublesome steam-powered machines, which enabled farmers to raise herd numbers. A new dairy factory was built to take advantage of the electricity. So it seems ironic that economic factors prompted the closure of the power plant, in 1975.

In the volatile economy of the 1920s, Six Mile was built "on the cheap". Old pipes that had brought water to local gold sluicing sites were recycled to bring water to the single turbine.

Most of the equipment was dragged to the site on horse-drawn wagons but Murchison's first motor truck also helped, the town's community newspaper says.

The paper raves that the "durable and trouble-free" power plant was "perhaps the best investment ever made by the Murchison County Council".

Peacock says Six Mile was part of a cluster of small but thriving communities up the Matakitaki Valley in the gold mining days. Earlier, diggers heading from Nelson and Blenheim to the West Coast trekked

Below: One of New Zealand's smallest hydro stations generated power for the Murchison district. The station building stands as a museum at Six Mile, situated "six miles" from Murchison town.

Below: The turbine in Murchison's Six Mile power station was fed by water pouring through recycled sluicing pipes from the goldfield. The station brought electricity to the remote area before many towns gained it. The development boosted dairy farming as electric milking machines allowed farmers to run more cows.

Right: The Waipori River tumbles down a steep gorge before joining the Taieri River near Henley and winding through coastal hills to the sea. Damming of the river on the plateau above the Taieri Plain created Lake Mahinerangi. Dams like this one in the gorge were added to the hydro scheme.

Bottom: Almost hidden in a cleft in rugged hills is the Waipori power station, built to generate electricity for Dunedin City. A village nearby housed workers on the station as access was only by road – and some road that was!

through here. They crossed the Maruia Saddle, which leads through the hills to the Shenandoah Valley.

A fair-weather "road" still runs over the Maruia Saddle. Leaving Six Mile in August, 2012, I decide to try the saddle in a *Press* car (a Kia Rio). It is a scary drive but I manage it – though I never boast of it within earshot of the editor or the fleet manager.

Dunedin citizens were demanding electricity early last century. The result was the Waipori hydro scheme, developed and run by the Dunedin City Council from 1907.

The Waipori River rises in the Lammerlaw Range. It makes the steep tumble from a tableland high above the Taieri Plain. It then pours across the plain and joins the Taieri River near Waihola. The enlarged river slips through coastal hills to the sea at Taieri Mouth.

I drive to Berwick, at the southern end of the Taieri Plain, in 2012. The road from there twists and turns on its 17 kilometre climb beside the river, beneath dripping bush, to emerge on the tableland. At the top is a 12 kilometre-long body of water, Lake Mahinerangi.

Prospectors were still living and working alongside the Waipori River on this bleak plateau when the council decided to dam the river and form the lake to hold water for a power plant.

First there was one dam. Then there were more. Now the Waipori scheme consists of four dams.

Rising waters from a new and higher dam in the 1920s forced the diggers and their families to leave. They did, but under protest. I go back in 2015 and meet local historian David Still and farmer Russell Knight there. They show me where the miners' lonely homes and the former town of Waipori Junction were flooded by the enlarged lake in 1925.

Proponents of the hydro scheme were quick to note that gold mining was benefitting from the first dam as it provided electricity for the dredges working in the area.

Having lived through the era of protest against the raising of lake levels for power stations at Manapouri and Clyde, and various other schemes that were halted by protestors, I find it interesting that such protest is by no means new. Interesting, too, is the fact that Dunedin City required a special Act of Parliament to allow the dam building to proceed.

After going to such trouble, the worthy Dunedinites must have felt crestfallen when the new dam was commissioned in 1923 but was immediately found to be unsafe. It had to be demolished. A replacement dam was built a short distance downstream.

That was not the end of the troubles dogging the Waipori scheme. When heavy rain fell in the Lammerlaws, power authorities had to release flow from the dams, lest they burst. The sudden rush of water down the Waipori River further saturated the already sodden Taieri Plain and increased the volume of the already overflowing Taieri River.

I can recall the old State Highway 1 hugging the coastal hills on the eastern side of the Taieri Plain, up to the 1960s. I can still see the sea of water that surged across the plain when the Taieri River flooded. When a new motorway was planned, down the centre of the plain, it required a huge amount of earthworks to raise the road above the flood level.

About 30 families lived in the hydro station village of Waipori Falls until the 1970s. The road beside the river made commuting from Dunedin or Mosgiel difficult. The road and the vehicles on it are much improved and the houses are now mostly weekend getaways.

Kayakers use the steep section of the Waipori River for training and competing. Anglers drive the road to get to their favourite fishing spots along Lake Mahinerangi, although easier access is possible from the

Outram-Middlemarch road and from Lawrence.

Like the citizens of Dunedin, Christchurch people demanded a reliable source of electricity. In 1914, they got it.

The Lake Coleridge power station might have come seven years after Dunedin got its Waipori station but it was the first in New Zealand to be built and operated by the state. It is now owned and operated by TrustPower.

The Lake Coleridge site, above the north bank of the Rakaia River in the alpine foothills, was chosen in preference to a strong proposal for a dam in the Waimakariri River gorge, near Sheffield.

Water flows into Lake Coleridge from the Wilberforce, Acheron and Harper rivers. The power station sits on an open slope below the lake. Large penstocks bring water down the slope to the turbines. The "spent" water is then released into the Rakaia River.

Although access from Christchurch is easy, the distance meant a sizeable village was needed for the workers. The houses remain and new ones have been added in recent years. Many are used by city people as holiday homes but about 30 people live here permanently. Bruce and Barbara Simpson, whom I meet there in 2011, are typical. They left Christchurch when Bruce was made redundant from his printing firm about 1990.

The Simpsons love it here. Barbara says the lifestyle is "addictive". It has been common for city folk to buy former power station houses for baches, then move in permanently as soon as they could afford to retire, she says.

Below: The power station village at Lake Coleridge, Central Canterbury, became a haven for Bruce and Barbara Simpson, of Christchurch. The couple love the relaxed lifestyle among the trees of the station's noted arboretum.

She and Bruce realise the importance of all the locals "pitching in" to sustain village life. Bruce has long been active in the volunteer fire brigade and Civil Defence.

One of the attractions is an expansive arboretum, which was started by station supervisor Harry Hart in the 1930s to relieve the bare, exposed landscape. Now in its maturity, the arboretum features thousands of conifers representing more than 140 species. Some of these, and some other types of trees found here, are rated as threatened and endangered species around the world.

Sign-posted walking paths weave their way through the arboretum on its various slopes and plains and down to the monolithic concrete power station that looks like something out of Stalinist Russia.

The 100 village families that lived here up to the 1960s have long gone. Tradesmen no longer raise a buzz of industry in depots, workshops and stores. The village has lost its school, so the few local children now attend classes at the aptly named Windwhistle. The mobile grocery shop no longer calls, so cars run down to Darfield for the weekly provisions. The Midland bus has not tooled down to Christchurch each morning and battled back into the nor'wester each evening for many years.

But the village has gained in other ways. It has taken on the appearance of an alpine tourist resort, complete with a tourist accommodation lodge in the former single workers' hostel. And yet, in accordance with the wishes of residents, it has not become afflicted with the hustle and bustle of commercialism.

I go back to Lake Coleridge in 2015 and find the attractive split-level village with its million-dollar mountain views has gained something else too – a sense of its history and a respect for its heritage.

I meet local women Karen Meares and Lyn Nell who sparked a small action group to lead centennial celebrations in 2014. Meares has lived and farmed near the lake all her life. Nell came here 40 years ago. Both are keen to promote the tourism potential of the area. They see heritage as a key to this, along with camping, fishing, scenery and relaxation.

Much of the heritage is based on the building of the dam. No one now remembers that, but searches by Meares, Nell, village resident Hugh Derham and power station worker Hugh Foster have found pictures, reports and memorabilia from the old power station that have been put on public display.

The display, designed and erected by Foster, helps visitors gain a feel for the old days. It evokes the rumble of iron wheels on gravel and the whiff of coal smoke billowing from steam traction engines as they hauled wagons bearing huge penstock sections from the railhead at Coalgate to the new power station.

Right: Large penstocks bring water at a great rate from Lake Coleridge to the power station far below. When the water has done its work spinning the turbines, it is discharged into the Rakaia River, to flow past Mt Hutt and onto the Canterbury Plains.

Reports from Derham's research can alarm visitors and cause them to quiver at the clatter of small stones pelting against the corrugated iron walls of workers' huts in violent wind storms.

Derham says the workers were kept awake at nights by this din. Their sleeplessness influenced Hart to start planting his arboretum in this treeless place. A century later we can enjoy the verdant village of Lake Coleridge as another of the benefits of electricity.

CHAPTER 11

Decline and fall

WALK THE STREETS of Tuapeka Mouth and feel the spooky chill in shadows cast by ancient trees. For Tuapeka Mouth is a ghost town. Here spirits whisper their secrets from sun-bleached walls of deserted houses.

The South Island has many towns that feel ghostly. Most began as gold mining settlements. I have heard the simpering of spirits amid the schist at Bendigo. I have seen long-bearded faces in mists ascending at St Bathans. I have shivered to a bagpiper's lament at Bannockburn. I have trod ground rumpled by miners restless in their graves at Charleston. I have sought signs of life in No Town – but even the ghosts have abandoned it.

Some gold towns found reasons to survive. Arrowtown became a tourist attraction and dormitory for Queenstown. Ophir is a retirement haven and stopover for cyclists on the rail trail. Ngahere remains the social and service centre of a dairy farming area. A few gold towns still produce gold – Ross, Macraes Flat, Reefton. Others declined but refused to die – Naseby, Kumara, Waikaia.

But enough of gold towns. Many solid little farming towns have declined too. Which brings us back to Tuapeka Mouth. Though it is situated beside a famed gold mining river, it was not a gold town. It stands well downstream from the Tuapeka diggings. It was a farm service town that owed its existence to the Clutha River punt service.

The decline of country towns that I pass through on trips to gather Heartland material prompts memories of my childhood in Hawarden, North Canterbury. It was a busy township then; it's a sleepy hollow now. Its decline is saddening.

Writing the Heartland columns for *The Press* has taught me that many readers share a sense of regret and loss at the decline of small towns. Columns on diminishing towns consistently draw the greatest response from readers. This was first noted with the column on Morven, near Waimate.

Past the last Waimate turnoff, heading south, I take a side road towards the sea in a 2008 trip. And here is Morven – not a ghost town, but a once well-dressed town now stripped of its former glory.

Grand old buildings gaze vacantly on Morven's empty main street like forgotten mannequins. Their paint peeled and fading, they stand shamelessly naked. But no one cares. There is no one on the street the day I call.

Opposite: Yesterday's vehicle and yesterday's building in yesterday's town – Morven, South Canterbury. The abandoned 1950s Austin pick-up truck shares its fate with the town's main street, though some life continues in other parts.

A clapped-out car sits under the veranda of a two-storeyed shop. Round the corner, cars that once gleamed in showrooms now rust in the grass that reaches above their hubcaps. Signs that were painted proudly on the walls of business premises can barely be read. With some difficulty I can just decipher the words on one: "cycles, drapery and ironmongery". I can pick out enough letters on other buildings to identify a butchery and a bakery. Other former shops leave me no clues. Down the road an imposing church building has been reduced to a glorified pigeon loft. No services have been held here for many years.

Morven is not dead. Rather, it appears to be stranded, like a derelict dinghy on a wide beach. The highway flashes by a few kilometres to the west. Trains rumble past without stopping. There is nothing to stop for. The only action I see is at the school, which is still open. A few houses are lived in. The Presbyterian church, the hall and sports ground look as if they are still used.

Morven was once on the scale of Wyndham, in Eastern Southland. Decaying buildings line Wyndham's main street too but the town is still humming when I visit in 2012. The huge Fonterra dairy factory at nearby Edendale, one of the world's largest, may contribute to Wyndham's survival. Factory workers can buy houses cheaply in Wyndham and make the short commute each day for work.

New dairy factories have opened within commuting distance of Morven too, at Studholme and Glenavy. They may be too small and it may be too late.

A Waimate man I meet remembers when Morven was much more. The South Canterbury Farmers Cooperative ran a big branch store and agency here. It was the sort of establishment that sold everything, from baked beans to gumboots, and it drew shoppers from miles around.

Irish families settled here when the big estates were broken up in the 1890s and early 1900s, he says. The town had a Catholic church with an imposing convent building and school, as well as the state school. As a Waimate schoolboy he played rugby against Morven. He discovered the hard way how pride in one's hometown can turn normal players into champions. There might have been some haggling between Catholic and Protestant kids but, oh boy, when they combined to represent Morven they were vigorously united.

Puponga was once the northern-most township in the South Island. It still would be, for it hasn't moved, but it is no longer a township.

Right: Rural decay: Visitors to Tuapeka Mouth are advised to beware of ghosts. The farm service township above the confluence of the Tuapeka and Clutha rivers prospered when the Clutha River punt was an important transport link. Its terminal decline began after World War II.

And this dismays resident Trevor Climo. He is a builder and there is not much building going on at Puponga.

I drive up to the top of Golden Bay in 2008. The sight of a dozen houses nestled for shelter against low hills and stunted trees bent by constant winds off the Tasman Sea surprises me. This is Puponga. This is the end of the tarseal. From here, Farewell Spit begins its long, gentle crescent curve across the bay.

Climo says only a handful of the homes are occupied. That is less surprising to me. For what would draw people to live in such a place? Peace and quiet? Certainly. Sea views? Yes. Boating and fishing? Sure. The new cafe that caters for tourists visiting the Spit? Okay. Jobs on dairy farms to the south of Puponga? Maybe.

Greater than all of these attractions, though, was coal. Mining of coal in the hills behind Puponga began in the 1890s, Climo says. A narrow gauge railway, first with wooden rails, then iron, was laid to cart coal from the mine to the coal company's wharf at the inlet. From there colliers crossed Golden Bay and Tasman Bay to carry coal to Nelson.

The nearest town was Collingwood, 40 minutes to the south by horse. That was too far for mine workers, so a township was established here. It grew considerably bigger than the cluster of houses that I see now.

The coal trade was short-lived. The mine closed in 1918, though it re-opened a little later. The wharf collapsed in 1943, causing a second closure of the mine. The wharf was not rebuilt but the mine opened again after World War II, when the road and improved trucks allowed transport by land to Collingwood. The whole operation ended in 1974.

The Climo family has been living here for several generations. Trevor remembers the vibrancy of the township when the Puponga mine and a rival mine only a kilometre away employed several hundred workers. He talks with animation about a childhood exploring the remains of house ruins and digging up all sorts of artefacts. He tells with dismay how later generations of teens have had to leave the district for study and jobs.

He is one of the few who came back. He finds enough work in building, repairs and maintenance around the wider area to keep him here. As he looks across the inlet, his eyes settle on rotting piles of the old wharf and ragged bits of metal left over from the little railway system, and his thoughts turn to all the people he knew who have gone from Puponga. Then he smiles with delight, suddenly recalling that

Left: Nothing stirs down the main street in Morven, an almost forgotten town that was once thriving. Rural towns everywhere have declined but the decay in Morven, South Canterbury, seems to highlight its former grandeur.

his son plans to return out of sheer love for the place.

Coal must take its place alongside gold as a leading player in the rise and fall of South Island country towns. A visit to Millerton, north of Westport, in 2006 illustrates for me the magnitude of coal's influence on our history. All through North Buller, all through the 20th century, coal was king.

An old friend from Millerton, Mel Douglas, loves to tell the story of a famous soccer team, the Millerton All Blacks. Many of the early Buller miners were British immigrants with mining backgrounds who brought the round ball game with them to rugby-mad New Zealand. They formed teams and launched competitions.

What colour do you associate with coal miners? Black, of course. Faces and hands blackened with coal. So Millerton named its soccer team, with tongue in cheek, the All Blacks. They might have remained largely unknown except for one thing. They were good. They won so many matches they entered the national Chatham Cup club championship and even reached the final one year.

So, says Douglas, if you enter a quiz and are asked how the All Blacks came to be playing in a national soccer final, that's the answer.

Douglas adds that soccer "caught on" at Millerton. He remembers many miners played both soccer and rugby, just as he did as a lad. He recalls some torrid battles on the Millerton domain. When things got too hot, or the players just got too tired, some thoughtful soul would boot the ball for all he was worth. It would fly far over the touch line, high above the crowd that lined the field and away down the hill. Then the players would sit down for a breather while keen kids scrambled after it and fought to be the one to find it among the bushes and trees far below the town.

All that is a distant memory for Millerton now. Brian Watson and John Green accompany me on my 2006 visit. Watson was born in Millerton and worked in the mines here. He later took up school teaching. Green was a miner at nearby Denniston and has charted the history of Millerton. He remembers a strong rivalry between the two communities – so close "as the crow flies", yet so far apart on their respective high and isolated plateaus where access through their mining period was difficult.

Watson leads us on a walk down his memory lane, past a tunnel through which the cable railway carried the coal, beside a dam and water reservoir, to the coal-fired power station which generated electricity for the whole town. The power went off at 10pm when the boilers were shut down, so you had to have spirit lamps and candles ready, Watson says.

He points out the sites of establishments he remembers: doctor's surgery, general store, butchery, two pubs, hall, theatre, three churches, sports facilities, several cottages. He takes us through the concrete remains of the extensive bath house where the blackened miners washed themselves down after a day at the coal face.

Millerton had a primary school. There were four teachers for 180 children, Watson says. Secondary students had to take the bus down the hill to Granity. Some went further, catching the train at Granity to attend Westport's Technical High School.

The streets we walk would form a grid pattern if they were on flat land. But this is undulating at best and riven with steep clefts at worst. Watson laughs as he explains – the town was planned in England, where the designers had no notion of the terrain, he says.

Mining at Millerton ended 50 years ago. The lively town dwindled sharply, even as the neighbouring Stockton mining area grew rapidly. I note the wide new road under construction to the Stockton Mine. It bypasses Millerton, seeming to shove this declining town into a page in the history books. I wonder if and when Stockton, too, will have "had its day".

Green has traced three stages of life in Millerton since mining ended. Firstly, "hippies' drifted in. These harmless, bearded types squatted in abandoned houses, strummed guitars and puffed on cannabis joints, Green says. Then a nastier brigade arrived – mean types with fierce dogs, they erected tall fences to conceal their drug dealing. In the most recent stage, artists, nature lovers and heritage preservers have moved in. They plug into the internet and Sky TV. Whatever their motivation, they bring life to a Millerton depleted of it.

Much the same drama has played out at another northern Buller coal town, Seddonville. But perhaps more than anyone else, one man has kept Seddonville ticking over. In 2011, I meet Dave Watson here. He is the recently retired proprietor of the hotel in a town so staunchly pro-Labour that a sign above the front door of a tidy little building announces the "H.E Holland Memorial Library". Harry Holland was the first leader of the New Zealand Labour Party.

Closure of the Charming Creek coalmine caused problems for Seddonville. The railway link with Westport was lost and people moved away. Fire added to the town's woes. It took a considerable community effort to save the place. Watson was chairman of most of the 17 community organisations, and on the committees of the rest. He was the top dog in mustering support.

Watson and his wife, Betty, had recently taken over the hotel from his parents, when it burned down, in 1975. Town stalwarts turned out to fight the fire but it was a lost cause, Watson tells me. They managed to wrench the beer cabinet from the wall and lug it outside.

Above: If something needed doing in Seddonville, Dave Watson was the man for the job. The publican in this Buller town was on a host of committees and chairman of most. While he fixed problems, his wife, Betty, ran the hotel. Now retired in Nelson, they return often for the whitebaiting.
Mike Crean, Fairfax Media NZ/ The Press

Little else was saved. Even the contents of the beer cabinet did not survive the rescue, Watson says with a knowing grin. Fortunately, most of the pub's beer stocks were securely locked in a separate, concrete building.

Regulations in those days required the hotel to be trading within 24 hours to retain its liquor licence. Watson was chairman of the town's hall committee. He arranged for the pub to set up in the hall, across the road. Volunteers helped carry crates of beer from the store lock-up to the hall. Pubs around Buller contributed jugs and glasses.

Meanwhile, members of the town's entertainment committee applied paint to smarten up the hall's dowdy appearance. And why not? Watson was chairman of the entertainment committee.

And, so, pub business resumed the next day. But there was a catch. The hall had been booked for a Seddonville reunion function a few days later. Watson handled that little dilemma too. You guessed it – he was chairman of the reunion committee as well.

Meanwhile, a new hotel was built in record time. It opened just 60 days after the fire. How was this achieved? Watson's network of friends and allies in high places, carefully nurtured through his multi-chairmanships, ensured plain sailing for the consents and permits required.

He was chairman of the school committee too. When the Education Board decided to close Seddonville School, Watson led the community campaign to take over the property and turn it into a motor camp. He succeeded and the camp is still running 20 years later.

Watson estimates about 100 residents still live in Seddonville. That is a fraction of the population he recalls from the bustling 1960s. Some have jobs in the remaining coal mines in the district, while others work on local dairy farms. So there is still a settlement here, though the hotel and camping ground are the only businesses in 2011.

Seddonville was never put up for sale, though Watson could probably have "done a deal" had he wanted to. The sign "Town for sale" did go up, however, at a town further south on the West Coast. Worldwide interest was generated by the chance to buy the town of Otira as a single entity.

Otira went into decline with the demise of steam locomotives on the Midland Railway Line, from the 1970s. The population dropped from 600 permanent residents to fewer than 50. High rainfall caused empty houses to become choked with prolific growth of weeds, grass and bushes. When I passed through the town on the Tranz-Alpine train in 1995, the commentator referred passengers to the magnificent gardens on the properties beside the railway. His sarcasm raised a few chuckles.

At its peak, Otira was a lunch stop for two express passenger trains a day between Christchurch and Greymouth. Catering for up to 200 hungry passengers in a tight time frame each day kept kitchen and serving staff busy. As steam trains did not go through the 8.5-kilometre-long Otira Tunnel, for fear of smoke suffocation, a fleet of electric locomotives was kept and maintained at Otira. Railway staff managed the station. Works gangs inspected, maintained and repaired running gear and track.

Below: Many towns have declined but few have been put up for sale. Former railway town Otira, now gathered around its hotel rather than its railway station, was one of the few. Solid ex-railway houses at knock-down prices and a small arts and crafts community keep Otira going.

When diesel replaced steam, the need for electric locomotives in the tunnel ended. Decreasing passenger loads led to the loss of all passenger services except the daily Tranz-Alpine, which had onboard catering services. Railway jobs at Otira were slashed. The coal-fired power station that supplied electricity to the railways and the town shut down. The school closed. The town lost its heart and its soul. It was put up for sale.

The town had been "transplanted" here when the tunnel opened in 1923. Its 18 railway houses had been prefabricated in Hamilton and transported by rail for assembly in this alpine setting. Seven decades later, they were emptied out. That's progress, but I wonder what the residents of the 1950s feel about it after all the frantic and unpaid work they did to strengthen stopbanks and save the town from several floods as torrential rain brought landslips rumbling down the hills and wild water encircled the town.

Christine and Bill Hennah of Auckland bought the town in 1999. Their new property portfolio included the 18 railway houses, the hotel and a few other buildings. When I visit in 2011, they have let 15 of the houses and are running the hotel. They have renovated it and added a cafe, store and postal agency.

But it is a struggle for them. Tenants come and go. Drink-driving laws have hit the bar trade. New facilities at Arthurs Pass township are drawing potential customers away from them. Frequent heavy rain is taking its toll, though the Hennahs insist Otira gets more dry days than Auckland.

They enthuse about the annual blooming of rata trees that turns surrounding hillsides into a wall of red. A few resident artists and craftspeople add their own colour, especially at the weekly market in the former town hall, the Hennahs say.

Whatever the advantages of living between a railway and a highway that bring them little custom, the Hennahs want to retire back to Auckland. They are ready to leave a life in the shade of towering mountains, under clouds menacing with moisture, to someone else. They have put Otira up for sale again.

Canterbury's pioneering Deans family sold a small part of their Homebush Station to William Waddington in 1873. The new owner showed his astuteness in establishing a village there. The village, which bears his name, grew into a significant town in the late 1800s and continued well into the 20th century.

Few people today know anything about Waddington. Does this indicate yet another example of rural town decline? After chatting with residents Dee and Jim Nunan in 2011, I am not so sure.

Waddington had the great advantage of sitting on the meeting place of several major roads and the Midland (Christchurch to Greymouth) Railway, between the townships of Darfield and Sheffield.

The railway reaches Waddington almost at the very spot where the Old West Coast Road and the current State Highway 73 converge. The former is still a busy access road to and from Christchurch. The latter continues to the West Coast via Arthurs Pass.

These two roads seem to form an arrowhead for which the historic Tramway Road is the shaft. Horse-drawn wagons carted coal from the Malvern Hills mines down Tramway Road in a straight line to the Main Trunk railway at Rolleston before the Midland Line was formed.

Cutting across these roads at Waddington is the well named Inland Scenic Route. Running along the baseline of Southern Alps foothills from Oxford to Geraldine, it crosses the Waimakariri River just north of Waddington. The bridge for this crossing was once shared by the railway line from Oxford to

Sheffield, which is only two kilometres from Waddington.

No wonder, then, that Waddington prospered. The Nunans have studied its history and found it once sported a range of shops, including butcher, baker, shoemaker and general store. It had a hospital and an undertaker (not necessarily associated), a blacksmith a wheelwright, a school and at least one church.

The Methodist Church was carted from Christchurch by bullock wagon in 1875 and services were held in it for 80 years. The church building was then used as a bunkhouse for the St John Ambulance training camp but was later sold and converted to a private home. The Nunans now live in the former parsonage. The school, which was closed after a new school was built at Sheffield in 1949, became the St John Ambulance camp.

All the commercial and social establishments have gone. So, yes, it does sound like the decline of a rural town. But the Nunans have noticed a different trend in the 20 years since they left Christchurch to live in tranquil Waddington. More and more city people have made the same move. Some, like them, are retired. The majority, though, commute daily as far as Christchurch for work.

The population of Waddington is stable at about 400, they say. That, combined with Sheffield's, is sufficient to ensure a strong community spirit. As for shops and services – the Nunans don't want any. Sheffield has a few shops, Darfield is progressive and growing rapidly and Christchurch is only 40 minutes away.

Decline? For a while, perhaps. But it has been reversed.

For true and definite decline, try Waterton. If you do an internet search of Waterton, you will not find much. The decline of this Mid Canterbury town, near the sea south-east of Ashburton, was complete and terminal.

However, your search may unearth a juicy bit of gossip. This refers to the mysterious death of Nunnia Mager, wife of Waterton Hotel proprietor James Mager. Nunnia, whose surname is spelt as Mauger on the headstone of her grave, was found dead from suffocation in 1884 at the age of 33.

James was accused of her murder but he denied it. He gave evidence to the court that she had been drinking heavily before her death. He was found not guilty. However, Waterton folk lore tells that James confessed to the deed on his deathbed.

The Magers had been married for 10 years but had run the hotel for only the last two of these. In that short time they had been in trouble with the police over unsavoury incidents on their licensed premises.

Very soon after Nunnia's death, James inserted an advertisement in an Ashburton paper saying the hotel had re-opened for business offering "the best accommodation", "liquors of the best brand" and "good stabling for horses".

Below: Dead centre: Graves in the cemetery at Waterton show this Mid-Canterbury town was once substantial. It is no more. Waterton was established as a dormitory town for workers on the Longbeach Station.

You may read into that what you will; I, of course, could not possibly conjecture. What is known, however, is that the hotel was sold later in that same year of 1884. It closed for ever in 1903 but nothing suspicious can be read into that. It happened that the Ashburton district voted for prohibition about that time. Waterton lived on, "dry", until its demise in the 1950s.

Alice McLaren asks me in 2011 if I have heard of Waterton. I have to shake my head ashamedly. Her forebears lived there and she wants fellow descendants to help erect a sign on the site of the former town. We are joined by local historian Gilmour Blee in a drive down to take a look at Waterton. We find there is nothing to suggest a town ever existed. There is a cemetery and in it we locate Mager's grave. But unkempt little cemeteries may be found in all sorts of places. We find a forlorn building that looks as if it might have been a woolshed. Blee says it was the Waterton Hall. It has almost certainly been used as a farm shed since its glory days. Blee says a sculptor was living in it in recent years but appears to have gone now. He points to a ditch that was once a water race that ran a few hundred metres eastwards to a flourmill. The mill has gone. And that's it.

But there was once much more, Blee says. Waterton was founded in 1876 to house some of the many workers and their families on John Grigg's Longbeach Estate. It was one of seven such townships in the wider area, of which few remain. It was surveyed for 139 residential sections, though Blee says probably only 20 to 30 houses were built. The population peaked at 120.

In addition to the hotel, Waterton had two churches – Anglican and Methodist. It had a shop and two blacksmiths. Waterton School was located a few kilometres south at the Longbeach farmstead. A daily coach service between Ashburton and Longbeach ran through Waterton, providing passenger, mail and freight services. Motor buses continued these services until the decline of Waterton in the 1950s.

Seeking another declining town, I come across another strange murder case – or two. McGregor Simpson and Pat Lewis show me around Arundel, on the north bank of the Rangitata River, near Geraldine. McGregor remembers his mother telling of how she heard a noise at 3am one night and looked out the window. She saw a man running across the paddock. Next day, neighbour Kathleen Rose was found dead in her bed from a gunshot wound. Her jilted lover later shot himself. Mrs Simpson gave evidence in what was judged to be a murder-suicide case.

That was at Arundel in 1931. The little town was rocked again six years later. Local resident Bill Gaby arrived home from collecting slops for his pig and found an intruder in the house. The burglar grabbed a stout manuka stick and belted 71-year-old Gaby over the head. Gaby dropped dead to the floor and the murderer escaped.

For this terrible deed the villain gained just £3 in cash and some lollies. His sweet tooth proved his undoing because, as he fled by train to Dunedin and then back to Timaru, he unwrapped lolly after lolly and carelessly discarded the wrappers. The police search turned into a paper chase that led to the killer's capture.

Arundel deserves to be remembered for more than murders. Like many a declining town, it was established at a popular river ferry crossing. The eventual building of a bridge over the Rangitata at this inland point caused the town's redundancy.

At its peak Arundel had two pubs, a store, a school, a post office, a hall, a race course and a sawmill. Almost nothing remains. Worse than that, across the road – the Inland Scenic Route – a massive irrigation scheme is starting to take shape when I visit in 2012. Giant earthmovers are annihilating any signs of part of Arundel to create a water storage lake.

There is a logic to this, as Simpson explains. The sacrifice of land on dry, hard country, for a lake equivalent in size to one farm will boost the growth of crops and pasture on many farms downstream. The net gain will be huge.

I accept this but it doesn't dull the little pang of regret I feel.

The Kowai County Council headquarters building stands alone and unused at Balcairn, between Rangiora and Amberley in North Canterbury. To see its statuesque whiteness in a plain of soft greens is to recall Percy Bysshe Shelley's poem, *Ozymandias*. This ode to the futility of human grandeur was a favourite of secondary school English teachers through the 1960s. The Empire loyalists who puffed on their pipes around the Kowai County Council table through the 1920s and 30s had probably not read it.

The South Island Main Trunk Railway runs through Balcairn. The selection of this route spelt the end of Leithfield as the principal town in the Kowai district, between the Waipara and Ashley rivers. Amberley at this early stage was not a contender.

Railway was king. Balcairn had the railway. Balcairn would be the county capital.

The council building was erected in 1922 and given the title of "Peace Memorial", in honour of local men who had fought in World War I. The town around it blossomed, but only briefly. The railway station busily managed transit of freight, livestock and passengers. The hotel had long been a coaching stop on the Rangiora-Amberley road. A blacksmith's shop stood next to it. A church, a school and a store were nearby. A hall was built in 1926. It is the only non-residential building in Balcairn still serving its original function. Some others have been converted to residences. They count among the dozen homes permanently occupied when I visit in 2013. A short distance away is the beautiful cemetery, now associated more with Amberley than Balcairn.

Local historian Graham Robertson shows me the "upping stone". This concrete block with steps on one side was used first to aid passengers boarding and alighting from buggies and coaches. It then became used for the same purpose with trains. Balcairn folk in those days could board a train here at 8.20am, spend a day in Christchurch and return on the 5.30pm train, Robertson says.

The railway station closed after World War II as road transport became increasingly popular. The main road was then re-aligned to allow traffic to sweep heedlessly past the village.

The diminishing settlement of Balcairn has languished on a sleepy side street since the 1950s. As home to a handful of serene retirees and other escapees from the city rat-race, it is as much a peace memorial as the grand council building itself.

The council building meanwhile has withstood all the changes. Ignoring the fact there is no longer a council, no longer even a Kowai County, it stands in a sort of meek defiance of all that has gone on around it. In a 2013 Heartland column I compared it to "the last skittle standing in a bowling alley". Not a bad description really.

A different sort of grand building stands aloft in Ngapara. From its elevated site, the limestone block structure casts its august gaze over the diminished township that nestles cutely in the hills of North Otago.

Unlike Balcairn's council building, Ngapara's former Railway Hotel is still in use when I drive up the hills from Duntroon and descend into this pretty valley in 2012. Neither does it look out of place. For almost opposite it is a building that hits a first-time visitor between the eyes. The former Ngapara flour mill is a massive limestone edifice, three storeys high in part, two storeys in the rest.

Together, the two buildings of an earlier age proclaim that the town you have just reached is a place of substance. Or was. For Ngapara today is the proverbial "blink and you'll miss it" village. My advice is, don't blink. This place is worth seeing.

Opposite: There's life in Balcairn yet. A train storms northwards through the little town on the South Island Main Trunk, near Rangiora. Balcairn has declined since its days as headquarters of the former Kowai County Council. The former council building is at right-rear.

Above: Not much is left of Ngapara but what there is looks impressive. Long ago the sun-drenched North Otago hills turned gold with waving wheat and Ngapara's mill produced train-loads of flour for export through the port at Oamaru. No one sows wheat any more. The railway has closed. The mill is Ngapara's memorial – in pure Oamaru limestone of course.

The former hotel is now a private house. The flour mill closed in 1973 but now operates again, though in a reduced form. Its huge grinders turn grain into a powder for mixing with other ingredients to produce stockfeed pellets.

Retired shearer and small farmer Roger Newlands was born here. As a lifetime resident he has taken it on himself to learn about the town's history and pass it on to anyone interested. He tells me the key to Ngapara's existence is a seam of coal that was discovered in a hillside one kilometre east of the town site by the pioneers. North Otago was a big grain farming area then but lack of coal to power steam engines limited the size of flour mills. Ngapara capitalised on its advantage by building this mammoth plant.

The mill attracted the railway which ran from Oamaru until 1959. For much of its life, the railway extended to the then busy Oamaru Port. Newlands says the mill was so big that the company imported grain from as far as Australia, via Oamaru Port, to supplement stocks from farms all over North Otago and parts of South Canterbury.

The flour mill recorded a bumper year in 1879, when 1000 bags of grain a day were unloaded from railway wagons during the season. Newlands remembers three trains a week bringing grain to Ngapara and taking flour back to Oamaru as late as the 1950s. Changes in farming and the centralising of flour milling in big towns from about that time started the decline of Ngapara.

Ngapara's Railway Hotel, as with Railway hotels in many rural towns, provided accommodation for travellers by train. It stood at the terminus of the Ngapara branch line, catering for people making long journeys, by horse or on foot, to and from places further inland. Dinner, bed and breakfast, not to mention a few drinks, at Ngapara would have been a welcome break for such travellers.

The first hotel burned down and the second was built, in the same position, in 1897. It closed only a decade later, when prohibition was voted in, Newlands says. The building was converted to a maternity hospital but that lasted only until 1912. It then became a grocery store. That business tailed off as people became more mobile and did their shopping in Oamaru. The building fell into disrepair until the current owners took it over, he says.

The mill, the hotel and the railway station formed the nucleus of the township for many years. As a railway terminus, the extensive stockyards and goods sheds were always busy. The town that grew up to serve the population included another hotel, a Masonic Lodge, three stores, a Post Office, a school and a hall. History has long pulled the shades on these but, just below the town I find a well tended rugby ground with swept-up clubrooms. So, local folk do have their priorities.

Newlands laughs. When he started playing rugby here, about 1950, the blokes all changed behind the gorse hedge, he says. A little later two huts were carted in and teams changed in them. They still had no showers, though, until a wooden shower block was built. The players thought this was very flash.

Then the present modern building was erected, "with every comfort and convenience".

"And now we don't even have a team in the senior grade," Newlands says.

People often ask me to name my favourite small town in the South Island. It's a tough task but if I am allowed to broaden the list of favourites slightly, I would certainly include Ngapara, along with a little village in the northern Catlins area called Romahapa.

Heading down to the Catlins I often notice sunshine glinting off rooftops away to the right of the main road, shortly before reaching Owaka. Rounding the next bend I see a sign pointing down a side-road to Romahapa. At last, in 2014, I find time to turn right there and explore this place. From first sight, it captures my heart. From learning more about its history, it takes my soul also. It is the ideal declining town to end this chapter.

The road dips into a deep defile surrounded by rolling hills. At rest in this narrow gap, where a lively stream burbles through, are the remains of Romahapa – perhaps 20 houses in various stages of decrepitude, sheltered by geriatric trees that have flourished in the area's high rainfall levels, a hall built in 1886 and modernised a century later, and a placid cow ruminating on a cracked and overgrown tennis court. Climbing out of the defile on the other side I reach the school and, just past it, the cemetery.

Can that be all? Of course not. At the school house I meet Shona Preddy, who has lived here for 22 years and drives the school bus. She lends me a copy of an article about Romahapa by local woman Ethel McLaren. From this I learn that Romahapa began as one of a cluster of tiny communities huddled around primitive mills that processed flax, twine, timber and flour in the mid 19th century. These settlements were separate but so close to one another that Preddy says she has never been able to identify exactly where one ended and another began.

Something brought them together, right here. And that something was the branch railway line pushing south from Balclutha. The line reached Romahapa in 1885. It eventually extended to Owaka and then continued south as far as Tahakopa, deep in The Catlins. As elsewhere in rural South Island, the coming of the railway boosted business and population in settlements along the line. At Romahapa it also drew the neighbouring settlements in, so that this town became a true "centre".

McLaren lists the railway station, a boarding house, a hotel, a smithy, a bakery, a butchery, a general store and a Post Office as resulting from the coming of the railway to Romahapa. All have gone but with a little imagination you can trace where the train tracks ran. As you drive through the defile, you notice a house at the bottom with a strangely slanting wall, uncomfortably close to the road. This was once the general store. Its shape was dictated by the alignment of the railway that passed almost within "spitting distance". From here you can just detect the slightly raised strips of land where the rails entered and left Romahapa, and the flat area where the station yards stood until the line closed in 1971.

Back on the hill, it is lunchtime at the school and I am amazed at the numbers of children rushing out to play. For such a small place, I expect a roll of about a dozen. Instead, Preddy tells me there are 55 pupils and three teachers. Then she admits the roll did slump as low as nine in the early 1990s and the school was facing possible closure.

Why the increase?

"People just keep coming," Preddy says. They have come from all over New Zealand and from England, Germany, South Africa, Canada, Scotland. Some work in Balclutha, 10 minutes away. Some work locally on farms. Yet I notice only half the old houses in the village seem occupied.

At the cemetery further up the hill Rev William Bannerman conducted the first church service in South Otago in 1854. This devout Presbyterian and his wife lived in a sod hut on the hill until a church and manse were built here two years later. The pioneers were true Scots and a mission hall was opened down in the village in 1908, debt free.

So much of Romahapa has gone and yet the child population is booming. It's a mystery. I can only put it down to divine intervention in this staunchly Presbyterian community.

These few are a fairly representative cross-section of declining townships. At first sight, they may seem to have little to offer, but they are rich in one aspect. Look below the surface and you find their decline serves to highlight their previous grandeur. That stirs nostalgia. And nostalgia can boost interest in history.

Below: The bend in the road through Romahapa was where the Catlins branch railway once crossed. The house at the corner was a shop. Romahapa was a busy township when flax and timber mills operated and daily trains stopped. The population has dwindled since, yet the school roll has swelled.

CHAPTER 12

Of this and that

No one could possibly mistake little-ol' me for a terrorist. Yet that was how I was made to feel one day while poking around Waimumu, near Gore in Southland.

My mission was to find something to write about in this lush, low hill country for the Heartland column in *The Press*. Pretty innocent, you might say. That was not how some official of the state-owned Solid Energy coal mining company saw it. I was stalked, confronted and virtually warned off looking at the company's open-cast lignite coal mine.

In 10 years of writing Heartland columns, my Waimumu Incident was the craziest experience of all. So it takes the lead in this chapter of sundry events, people and places of interest from those years.

Waimumu meant two things to me – Southern Field Days for farmers and coal mining. The coal mine there supplied us with cheap coal when we lived in Mataura, some 15 kilometres away, in the early 1970s. Lignite does not burn well in the open grate because of its high water content. But at least it does burn and it gives off some heat.

I remember the Commer truck of the New Vale Coal Company at Waimumu dumping loads of the stuff in our yard. New Vale sold out to Solid Energy in 2006. The new owner developed a huge open-cast operation that carved away at the hills to extract lignite for

Southland's milk factories and freezing works and for a new coal briquette manufacturing plant near Mataura.

So, on a 2012 Heartland trip in Eastern Southland, I decide to take a look at Waimumu. There is not much to look at. The 19th century town of 600 people was based on gold dredging and farming. All that remains is a school that appears to have been closed for several years and a church that looks little used.

This population downturn is reversed, however temporarily, every second year. Then the Field Days attract 30,000 people from all over Southland and Otago. It is the biggest event south of the Clutha River.

But back to the coal. This is a hot topic. Coal has become anathema to environmentalists because of its contribution to global warming and climate change and the despoliation of the landscape by mining. So you can understand why Solid Energy might be a little nervous about journalists suddenly popping up to look at their massive open-cast pit.

On arrival, I park in the public carpark and, having read the sign stating all visitors must report to reception, I enter by the appropriate

Opposite: At the end of the road is a place called Paradise. The track reduces to a trail where few people go, save keen anglers and adventurers. Paradise lies upcountry from Glenorchy, at the head of Lake Wakatipu.

door. A pleasant woman greets me and asks how she can help. I tell her I am writing a column for *The Press* on Waimumu and would like some information on the mining operation.

The good woman takes on a defensive demeanour and says I will have to ask Solid Energy's information staff, in Christchurch.

I suggest she might have some basic information sheets for visitors right here, on site. But no. She closes down abruptly. So I thank her for being helpful, without a hint of sarcasm, you understand, and return to my car.

Nowhere on the road to the mine or in the carpark or reception office could I see anything of the big mine. But I have a dim memory of a side road a little way past the main entrance, from 40 years ago. So I drive a short distance up the hill and, sure enough, there it is – a shingle road winding away to the left, over the brow of a hill. I take the road and, cresting the hill, see before me a wide-screen view of the open-cast mine, so big it dwarfs the trucks and loaders beetling around down there.

To get the best photograph possible, I climb on the roof of the car. Well, it is a company car, so it can take it. I click away on my camera, then continue my drive. At the bottom of the hill I reach a crossing where coal-laden trucks coming from the mine grind their way over the road and enter a yard where the coal is transferred to loading apparatus that pours the coal into road-going trucks. The crossing is stained black from wet coal slurry dripping from the trucks, like a smoker's fingers.

As I snap a few photographs of the loading depot, a Solid Energy utility vehicle pulls up in a cloud of dust beside me and a harassed look-ing man steps out. He approaches me and asks what I am doing.

Below: Old King Coal was a merry old soul – but not at Waimumu. Management of the Solid Energy coal mine near Gore was not happy to see this *Press* journalist snooping around. Did they have something to hide? No, they were just wary of adverse publicity and interfering protesters.

"Taking photos," I say, with all the naivety I can muster.

"Why are you taking photos? This is private land," he says.

"It is a public road and I am as entitled as anyone to take photos from a public road," I reply.

He hesitates and harrumphs before saying: "It is a public road now but it won't be for much longer. We are getting it closed".

"Oh," I say. "Do you have something to hide then?"

He sputters in the negative and I begin to feel sorry for him. He seems quite a nice chap, actually. So I explain my mission more fully. This cuts the ice and we both relax a bit.

He explains that I was being watched for a while before I came to this point. He then received a call about my movements and was told to intercept me and find out what I was doing. He adds, with disarming familiarity, that I don't seem to be a trouble-maker but the company is very wary of strangers since some environmental protesters chained themselves to mining machinery a while ago.

He assures me that Solid Energy will restore the ugly coal hole to first-class farmland when mining finishes and we part on good terms.

He seems relieved that espionage and vandalism have been averted. I am happy to have my photographs and my story, even if it is more about Solid Energy's wariness of terrorists than about the Waimumu coal operations. Never mind, I can get that stuff from their information staff in Christchurch. I know one of them quite well.

I always hesitated to take liberties with company cars but must confess to another instance when I drove a wee bit further than I would take my own humble hatchback.

It all began when my wife and I decided to pay the princely sum of $500 for an original oil landscape painting by Diamond Harbour artist Malcolm Mason. We did not have a grand original on any wall and we liked this one even if, at first glance we mistook the scene for the Otira Gorge. In his gentlemanly way, Mason corrected us. This was Paradise, a little known spot deep in the hills beyond Glenorchy, he said.

Finding out about Paradise spurred me to go there. What better way to manage such an expedition than to include it in a Heartland column on Glenorchy, the little settlement at the head of Lake Wakatipu which I had been to only once before?

The drive from Queenstown is a half-hour battle with winds whipping dust into great whorls that race across the landscape, until squalls of rain from billowing black clouds take over. But at Glenorchy the weather clears to leave a restless wind that wails from sullen mountains and sweeps down the valley of the Dart and Rees rivers as if through a funnel.

A taciturn local who calls himself Hubba says the river headwaters get the rain; Glenorchy is the wind tunnel. But he loves it. The small adventure tourist town has a history of farming, scheelite mining, and contact with the outside world by the celebrated steamer Earnslaw. It has a shop, a garage, a pub, a school and the sort of visitors who want to get off their backsides and head into the wilds.

Hubba says he and other modern settlers here have seen the world and not liked it much. This is their retreat. They are interesting people. This is the place for them. It is "the gateway to Paradise".

So I turn the car up the valley to this mystical Paradise. For a small community in a village with the feel of a Wild West frontier town, I see a surprising number of people: farm hands driving cattle, van drivers shuttling customers to their raft ride location, riders setting out on a horse trek. All wave with the friendliness of small places.

Past the end of the tarseal I go, around beautiful Diamond Lake, past palatial Arcadia homestead, through fords where water rushes up to my wheel hubs, below towering alpine vistas that soar steeply skywards.

As the road defaults to a track the landscape adopts an alien planet appearance without people. I must be near Paradise now. The track closes in ahead of me. It becomes a mere trail which would wrench the wheels and bump and scrape the bottom of the car. Time to turn back.

Returning to Glenorchy I call at the Department of Conservation office. A ranger there shows me on a detailed map how close I got to Paradise – a few hundred metres short.

Does it matter that I got so near to, and yet so far from Paradise? Not at all. For I have it already, in oils, framed, on my wall.

The Catlins area has become popular since sealing of the main road through it was completed 20-odd years ago. It has been a favourite of mine since first driving through in 1971.

A visit to the Catlins in 2014 produces a favourite moment for me as Heartland writer. At Owaka I renew acquaintance with the town's excellent museum director, Kaaren Mitcalfe. She tells me about the loss of Trans-Tasman liner Manuka on this so-called "Shipwreck Coast" in 1929. She shows me relics of the ship in the museum and suggests I chat to retired farmer John Burgess at Pounawea for more information.

A seven-minute drive takes me to Pounawea, a beach settlement above the lagoon at the junction of the Pounawea and Catlins rivers. Signs of old wharves can be seen where sturdy coastal vessels once tied up to load logs for the building of Dunedin homes.

Burgess works part-time as a volunteer helper at the Owaka Museum. He tells me about an elderly woman visitor who came into the museum a few years ago. The woman identified herself simply as one of the survivors of the Manuka. She was making a last trip to the Catlins and was touched to see a model of the ship and mementoes from it on display. She would love to revisit Long Point, south of Owaka, where the ship hit a reef and went down.

Burgess was interested and offered to take her there the next day, when he would be free to go. So, next morning he picked up the

Right: The Catlins Coast is also known as the Shipwreck Coast. SS Manuka, a trans-Tasman liner, was one of many vessels that foundered on rocks along the South Otago-Southland shores. Gael Ramsay of the Owaka Museum shows some of the items salvaged from the Manuka.

Below: This model of the ship is in the Owaka Museum.

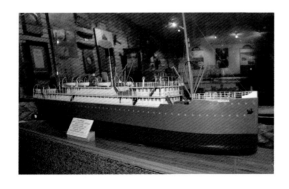

Above: "We were castaways," says Jean Hudson, reminiscing on her ordeal when trans-Tasman passenger ship Manuka went down off the Catlins coast in 1929. The 200 passengers and crew members bobbed about in lifeboats during the night, then landed on a remote beach. No one knew anything about it, Hudson says. Castaways indeed!

mother was convinced the "elderly woman" that Burgess mentioned was her. She was keen to tell me more about the shipwreck and its aftermath.

So I visit the 90-year-old Hudson in a Christchurch retirement home. Although she was only six when the Manuka went down, she recalls much of the ordeal with great clarity. She explains that her mother, with whom she was travelling home from a visit to Australia in 1929, often spoke of it, so some of her memories have been fleshed out by what she heard.

Hudson has long been dismayed that the Manuka incident has never captured as much public attention as other shipwrecks. She attributes this to the fact that all 200 passengers and crew members (plus a couple of stowaway shearers) survived. Had there been deaths, more would have been made of the event, she says. She recalls also her visit to Owaka and the kind Mr Burgess taking her back to the shipwreck site.

The Manuka sailed from Melbourne on its usual passage to Lyttelton, with calls scheduled at Bluff and Port Chalmers. A few hours after leaving Bluff, it struck the reef off Long Point late at night. The order was relayed to passengers to dress warmly. Then came the order to go to the lifeboats. Hudson remembers being passed from hand to hand by crewmen and placed in a boat that was already bobbing on the water. Her mother, meanwhile, descended on a rope ladder.

For five hours the boats were tossed on the heaving sea. She speaks with a shudder of seeing the ship's superstructure slip from sight behind large rocks and hearing the boom of its boiler exploding as it went under.

When light was sufficient to see clearly, they were rowed to a tiny beach. They clambered up to dry land and flopped onto the ground. Some crewmen climbed the cliff and went to seek help. A farmer going out to bring in his cows heard them. He alerted neighbours and the rescue was soon under way.

elderly woman and drove her the 35 kilometres south to Long Point. A short walk from the road provided a view of the reef and the strip of sand where she and her fellow survivors had huddled in the dark. It brought back memories for the woman. She told of straggling in the early daylight along the ridge to where a farmer had mustered some neighbours with trucks to take the castaways to Owaka. There a hot meal and dry clothes awaited them.

The Heartland column about Owaka and Pounawea ran in *The Press*, with photographs of the museum's model of the Manuka and Mitcalfe holding a porthole ring from the sunken ship. Soon after, I received a letter from a reader of the column who had heard her mother talk about abandoning the shipwrecked Manuka. She had cut out the column and shown it to her mother, Jean Hudson. Her

Hudson remembers riding on the deck of a truck to Owaka, where the community was organising a reception. The survivors were allocated to family homes where they were fed and given fresh clothes. Later in the day a special train that had been sent from Dunedin to fetch them arrived. Less than 24 hours after the alarm was sounded, the Manuka passengers were being greeted by well-wishers on the station platform at Dunedin.

Only one memory of what they did in Dunedin remains sharp for Hudson. She went with her mother to a Post Office to send a cable to her father telling him they were safe and well. They had just been visiting her father, who was in Tasmania in a temporary position as an agricultural adviser. He would later become director of Lincoln College, near Christchurch.

Hudson and her mother proceeded to Christchurch by train the following day.

Many a castaway has washed up on the Catlins coast. Possibly as many have washed up on Nelson's Boulder Bank. But the latter tend to be willing escapees from the competitive world of business. They are people seeking solitude, yearning for communion with the elements of sea and stones, wind and weather.

One such is Gilbert Inkster. The retired mariner had "sailed the seven seas" and found it difficult to settle down to life on land. After further years of working as a harbour pilot, dredge master and harbour master at Nelson, he still felt the tug of the wide and wild ocean.

When I meet Inkster in 2013, he has found peace at last amid homely comforts in a Nelson suburb. How can this be? His bach on Boulder Bank is the answer. It has been a bridge

for him. It has connected him with sea spray and raging surf on one side. On the other the still waters of Nelson Haven offer easy access to all he needs, he says.

Boulder Bank is a natural breakwater of stones that shelters the port and bay of Nelson. Its eight kilometre length almost encloses the bay. Ships used to negotiate the narrow passage between Haulashore Island and the western end of the bank. This gap was widened in 1906 to allow bigger vessels to enter and leave the port with ease.

Prominent on the bank is a century-old lighthouse. It stands like a nanny at the end of a straggling line of six (once there were eight) little shacks. These ad-hoc baches of colours gaudy and diverse have divided Nelsonians over the ages. Some say they are eyesores and should be removed. Others proclaim them

as endearing items of heritage. Bach owners lease their little patches of shingle from the Department of Conservation.

Inkster and his wife, Christine, bought their bach in 1968 from a World War II veteran who had built it for himself. The Inkster family used it frequently, not deterred by the isolation that forced the use of oil lamps for lighting, wood stoves for heating, gas cookers for preparing meals and tanks for carting fresh water from the mainland in their dinghy.

Above: They call it Shipwreck Coast, but few ships founder on the reefs and rocks of the Catlins any more. The South Otago shoreline has become a popular getaway for city folk and a magnet for surfers prepared to shiver a little.

Above: "Home is the sailor, home from sea" – but Gilbert Inkster's heart is still on the ocean waves. When he came ashore, at Nelson, he bought a bach on Boulder Bank. There he can feel the ocean's moods and motions on one side, and the serenity of Nelson Haven on the other.

Right: The rocky cliffs of Quail Island suggest a formidable stronghold exists here. But the island, in Lyttelton Harbour, is a popular picnic and leisure venue for all ages, easily accessible by regular ferry sailings. Its history and native flora are major attractions.

Opposite top: Old barracks building on Quail Island, in Lyttelton Harbour.

Opposite bottom: Ships' graveyard: Before the days of resource consents, obsolete sea craft were towed to a little-seen place and sunk. Such a spot is at the south-west corner of Quail Island, in Lyttelton Harbour. The remains of the sunken ships, now exposed, resemble the ribs of large animals whose flesh has rotted away.

Neither are they bothered by storms or the threat of a tsunami flushing the baches away. They even enjoy a good blow that flails the bach walls with salt spray and hurls high tides up to the door.

"We like the isolation. It's easy to get there by boat. There is the fishing, the quietness. The bird life is interesting," Inkster says.

"It is like being at sea without the motion of a ship. You can appreciate the weather changes, you're so exposed. It's a lovely place," he says.

Life on Boulder Bank would not be for everybody, Inkster admits, but he recommends a walk along the bank to get a "feel for it". So I try it and find he is right – in a way. Once my feet grow accustomed to crunching, tripping and sliding on stones, and when I get used to the wind in my hair, I begin to appreciate the uncanny contrast of crashing waves on one side and water as still as a mill pond on the other. And yes, I do enjoy it.

Another marine topic to appear in Heartland is Quail Island. Sitting in Lyttelton Harbour, it has had many uses, ranging from a quarantine station to a sheep farm, from a leprosy colony to a depot for Captain Robert Scott's polar expeditions, from a quarry supplying rock ballast for emigrant ships returning to Britain, to a graveyard for vessels that had passed their "use-by date". In latter years it has become a popular picnic spot for Christchurch folk, accessible from Lyttelton by ferry.

A century-and-a-half of wear and tear has taken its toll on the native trees and shrubs. Learning of a project to restore much of the island's vegetation, I take the five-minute boat ride there in 2013 with nature conservationists Ian McLennan and Tony Giles.

About 20 years have passed since my last visit to the island, on a family picnic. The changes wrought in the latter part of that time by Department of Conservation staff and volunteers with the Otamahua Quail Island Restoration Trust are striking. Formerly treeless slopes are now covered in native trees and plants that reach two metres and more into the sky.

Giles rejoices that these, and thousands of other native trees and bushes planted in the last six years, are already bringing kiwi, kereru (wood pigeon), tui and korimako (bellbird) back here to feed and nest.

"It [the island] will be a jewel for future generations," Giles says. Thousands of people visit each summer. They walk the tracks, examine the historic places and swim in the sheltered southern cove. School groups come to help with planting.

"If only more people would climb to the top and see the dramatic change," McLennan adds.

Once on the island, I feel a sense of "splendid isolation" from the cares and woes of life on the mainland. I quickly find this is an illusion. The Canterbury earthquakes of 2010-2011 flash back to mind at the sight of a leper's grave that slumped as the ground writhed and sank beneath it. I see the trunk of a giant macrocarpa tree lying contorted and bleached by sun. McLennan tells me the tree toppled in severe gales that wracked the island in the 1968 storm that drove steamship Wahine onto rocks in Wellington Harbour at the cost of many lives. I see predator traps, set to catch rabbits,

possums and stray dogs that swim from King Billy Island at low tide.

The native quail that gave the island its name became extinct early last century. Conservation efforts will go on forever to ensure no more native species go that way, McLennan says.

Dunback may, or may not, be a dying town. There is no doubt, though, it once had a close connection with death.

The East Otago settlement is the last remaining town on the Pigroot. It sits at the eastern end of this strangely named road that, long ago, stirred fear in the hearts of travellers.

This section of the highway from Palmerston to Ranfurly climbs through rugged hill country where wild pigs once rooted the earth for food with their tough noses and vicious tusks. However, it is not clear that this is the derivation of the name Pigroot. Some people say the

name derives from an old saying that the road was "a pig of a route".

In one of its deep ravines lie the bones of draught horses that heaved their last breath as they tugged heavy wagons up the steepest stretch on the trail. The faithful Dobbins were unceremoniously cut from the traces and rolled over the edge of the cliff to their grave far below.

The pub at Dunback did a roaring trade from the early 1860s as drovers and drivers took a well-deserved spell before, and after, negotiating the infamous Pigroot. Dunback was later the terminus of the branch railway from Palmerston, which delivered even more customers.

Don McLenaghen runs the historic pub when I call in 2012. He says one of the strange things about Dunback is that it has never had a cemetery. And this, he tells me, may be why it had a morgue in the old days.

To explain this, McLenaghen leads me outside and around to the back of the hotel. And there, in the brick wall, is something that, at first sight, looks like a window that has been boarded up.

But this is no window. It is set too low in the wall, less than a metre above the ground. McLenaghen says his inquiries into this ancient casement revealed it was a trapdoor through which dead bodies were pushed. The room on the inside of the trapdoor was a morgue.

Why did little Dunback have a morgue? In the Long Depression of the 1880s and 1890s, many unemployed men packed their swags, strung them on their backs and came through here seeking jobs, McLenaghen says. Swaggers trekked from farm to farm in search of a bed and a meal in return for a few hours of work chopping wood, digging gardens and the like. Others tackled the difficult road and came to grief on its steep and slippery slopes.

Mortality was high among them, he says.

Sadly, it was common for men to perish and be found by other travellers. It was equally common for the dead to have been carrying no identification and to be unknown to anyone locally. So their bodies were loaded onto farm drays and carted to Dunback – to the pub and the trapdoor leading to the morgue.

The undertaker at Palmerston was informed of a body awaiting burial and would take the train up to Dunback. The body would be transferred to the train and taken to Palmerston for interment in the cemetery there.

McLenaghen trembles a little as he adds that two ghosts haunt his hotel.

"I never believed in ghosts but I do now," he says. He tells me of staff and guests reporting strange happenings – footsteps in vacant rooms, handbags shifted from one table to another, a bed rising 500 millimetres and falling again, doors opening and shutting.

It could be imagination, of course. It could be a publicity stunt. Or it could be the spirit of a swagman unable to rest in peace after being jolted on a dray and shoved through the trapdoor to the morgue in the Dunback Hotel.

Whatever, the old pub is still going strong in 2012. The Pigroot is an easy drive these days so most travellers just barrel through the little township. But goldmining at Macraes Flat, 20 minutes away, ensures a flow of guests and lodgers at the landmark building.

And the morgue? McLenaghen does not use the room. Just in case it might upset the ghosts.

The 1931 hotel at Garston provides a different sort of story. It was built in graceful art-deco style and looks most impressive beside the highway that carries a stream of campervans and tour coaches between Lumsden and Kingston in Northern Southland.

This was a busy tourist route from early times when trains brought visitors to Kingston to catch a steamship that would take them up

Lake Wakatipu to Queenstown. Garston then had a busy railway station. An earlier hotel here burned down in 1930.

I met Sheryl and Bill Chisholm, proprietors of the present hotel in 2001. Passing by on a 2011 Heartland trip, I pop in to see if they are still here. Sadly, they have gone but their story remains a talking point in the township.

Locals love to tell you that the Chisholms relocated from Geneva to Garston. And that is correct, if a trifle ironic. Sheryl had been a New Zealand diplomatic representative at the United Nations headquarters in the Swiss city. Bill had "tagged along" and become a chauffeur to diplomats and ambassadors there.

This was indeed the "high life" but the Kiwi couple got sick of it. They yearned to return home and find a quiet spot to settle down. Back in New Zealand they toured the country seeking a pub for sale. They found the Garston Hotel and bought it in 1999. It was the only liquor outlet in a large area.

After my return visit in 2011, I trace Sheryl and phone her. She confirms these details, just as she had told me a decade previously. She adds that she and Bill decided to sell the hotel and leave in 2003 because it had become too busy.

Garston – a pub, a school and a gallery – too busy? I can hardly believe it. So Sheryl explains the events of their time in the southern town.

The Chisholms were clobbered by "a triple whammy" in their first 18 months there, she says. A host of job losses on farms and in forestry slashed patronage at the bar. A boost to policing drink-drive laws in rural Southland deterred people from going to pubs or functions where alcohol was served. And the store at Atholl, a slightly bigger township 12 kilometres away, gained a licence to sell beer, wine and spirits.

Business at the Garston Hotel suffered but the Chisholms did not give up. They had two cards to play. The first was to attract rich American anglers to Garston to fish in the headwaters of the nearby Mataura – "the best trout fishing river in the world". This worked and soon wealthy Americans were paying for upgraded accommodation and excellent dining, leaving generous tips, and coming back again.

Secondly, regulations limiting the hours truck drivers could stay at the wheel meant long-haul drivers were looking for overnight stays with solid dinners, cooked breakfasts and cut lunches to take away. The Chisholms met these needs and the drivers spread the word among their colleagues. Garston became a recognised truck-stop.

Below: Dunback Hotel, beside the Pigroot road in East Otago, is said to be haunted. Could it be that the spirits of unidentified swagmen who died and were dumped in the morgue at the rear of the hotel are causing strange noises and inexplicable happenings deep in the night?

Business boomed again. No wonder it became all too much for a couple seeking a peaceful life in a quiet place.

The Chisholms sold the hotel to furniture restorer Tony Sparks in 2003. Sparks later resold the hotel but kept the old stone stables building and converted it into a house. He also bought the former garage across the road and converted it into a gallery and workshop. There he displays and sells restored furniture, art and craft items and local produce.

Before I leave, I buy some honey that has come from a local hive. It has a beautifully pungent flavour. I see a few cars stop but not enough to ensure brisk trade. A customer says the little community hopes a buyer for the Kingston Flyer vintage excursion train from Kingston will extend the rail ride a few kilometres from its Fairlight terminus to Garston. This would provide more potential customers but I fear the chance is slim.

My greatest surprise in 10 years of travelling South Island roads for Heartland was probably discovering a monument to a "massacre" that occurred more than 300 years ago on the opposite side of the world. After researching the topic and running a column on it in *The Press*, I received angry calls and letters from readers whose ancestors had been associated with the historical event. The depth of bitterness that some people hold in their hearts surprised me.

The monument stands near the road that undulates over some of the best farming country in New Zealand, between Winton and Mataura in Southland. Cruising along this road in 2009, I notice a high cross on a tall stone plinth in the middle of a farm paddock. By the roadside an iron gate hangs from a pair of stout stone posts. On the gate is a sign with the name Glencoe in Gaelic-style lettering.

I enter and approach the monument. The inscription reads: "In memory of the early settlers of this Glencoe, of which many were McDonalds".

The monument was erected by Clan Donald of Southland. It commemorates the killing in 1692 of 38 McDonalds (or MacDonalds) near Glencoe in Scotland, and the deaths of a further 40 from wounds, starvation and exposure.

McDonalds refer to the killing as a massacre by a feuding rival clan, the Campbells. Other clans see it differently. You can read in the history books about this fiery period in Scottish history, following the Jacobite Uprising, when clans clashed in the contest for supremacy. Then you can make your own judgment.

Whatever you decide, I advise against trumpeting your view, lest you be damned by some clan descendant, as I was when Glencoe, New Zealand, featured in a Heartland column.

Ah well, touring the South Island and writing Heartland columns was a rare pleasure. A few angry phone calls and letters could not mar that.

Opposite: What could be more peaceful than a farm paddock in the heart of Southland's rolling hill country? And yet, this monument beside the road between Winton and Mataura recalls the savagery of clan warfare at Glencoe, Scotland, more than 300 years ago.

Index

Timber was scarce in Central Otago as few trees flourished in the extremes of the region's climate. But schist was abundant, so the pioneers built in stone. The hills of Bendigo, north of Cromwell, are partly covered in grape vines now but remnants of mining settlements remain scattered across the former goldfield.

With rocks looming from the surf like small islands, the Catlins Coast can be a navigator's nightmare. The south-east corner of the South Island was dubbed Shipwreck Coast in the days when small vessels provided the main form of communication to isolated farms. Many craft foundered here, among them the trans-Tasman passenger liner Manuka, in 1929. The rocks pictured are just south of Nugget Point, in the Catlins district.